Job Interview

How to Mindfully Prepare for Your Job Interview

(Interview Secrets That Employers and Headhunters Don't Want You to Know)

Charles Pack

Published By **George Denver**

Charles Pack

All Rights Reserved

Job Interview: How to Mindfully Prepare for Your Job Interview (Interview Secrets That Employers and Headhunters Don't Want You to Know)

ISBN 978-1-7382957-1-5

No part of this guidebook shall be reproduced in any form without permission in writing from the publisher except in the case of brief quotations embodied in critical articles or reviews.

Legal & Disclaimer

The information contained in this book is not designed to replace or take the place of any form of medicine or professional medical advice. The information in this book has been provided for educational & entertainment purposes only.

The information contained in this book has been compiled from sources deemed reliable, and it is accurate to the best of the Author's knowledge; however, the Author cannot guarantee its accuracy and validity and cannot be held liable for any errors or omissions. Changes are periodically made to this book. You must consult your doctor or get professional medical advice before using any of the suggested remedies, techniques, or information in this book.

Upon using the information contained in this book, you agree to hold harmless the Author from and against any damages, costs, and expenses, including any legal fees potentially resulting from the application of any of the information provided by this guide. This disclaimer applies to any damages or injury caused by the use and application, whether directly or indirectly, of any advice or information presented, whether for breach of contract, tort, negligence, personal injury, criminal intent, or under any other cause of action.

You agree to accept all risks of using the information presented inside this book. You need to consult a professional medical practitioner in order to ensure you are both able and healthy enough to participate in this program.

Table Of Contents

Chapter 1: Job Searching...................1

Chapter 2: Employment Groups Are Unique............................20

Chapter 3: The Course of the Interview 34

Chapter 4: Revealing Truths Approximately 53

Chapter 5: Trick Interview Questions69

Chapter 6: New Task 80

Chapter 7: Understanding the Interview Process 83

Chapter 8: Preparing For the Interview 94

Chapter 9: Crafting Effective Responses 106

Chapter 10: Communication Skills and Body Language 117

Chapter 11: The Day of the Interview128

Chapter 12: Navigating Special Situations 138

Chapter 13: Advanced Interview Techniques 149

Chapter 14: Preparing For the Interview 161

Chapter 15: Presenting Yourself ... 180

Chapter 1: Job Searching

Job searching can be a hard and overwhelming undertaking because of the various resumes you should ship out and the countless undertaking applications that you have to fill out. However, generation has made it much less complicated than ever to search for a undertaking, observe, and observe up with the employer. Now more than ever there are various strategies that a person can practice to a procedure. They can use on-line system boards, visit a business enterprise's net net site, attend a venture trustworthy, or move from business enterprise to commercial agency and ask about interest openings. There isn't any wrong way to look for a assignment. Whichever method you pick out, honestly make sure which you devote enough time during the day or night to look for a technique. Usually, it is recommended which you spend anywhere from 2-3 hours an afternoon searching out a method. In this next segment, I skip over truths about procedure searching. These are maxims that people might not be aware of but want to be as it will make their project seek go smoother.

Revealing truths approximately pastime looking.

Job descriptions are idealistic so don't worry if you don't meet all of the requirements.

Job descriptions aren't written by using the real employees acting the undertaking. The truth is that they're written with the resource of human beings that are not acquainted with the interest itself. In addition to this, interest descriptions are written with the motive of attracting the pleasant candidate but there can be no such individual. There might be a handful of people that can perform maximum of the duties however there isn't always one unmarried character that would do all of the obligations. I let you know this, so that you received't experience intimidated or awful in case you don't have all the skills or that a whole lot enjoy. The crucial trouble to consider is in case you apprehend the way to do 30% of the system, then exercise. I say 30% due to the reality those are the fundamentals of the undertaking. The particular 70% you can have a look at on the procedure. I have worked with severa customers that did now not follow to jobs due to the reality they believed that they did no longer have the ok competencies or enough revel in to do the mission. But with the beneficial resource of doing so, they take themselves out of the taking walks for the area. Therefore, while you look at a manner posting, ask your self, can I do this mission? And if the solution is positive, then follow! You do no longer have something to lose, and the whole thing to advantage.

Age is truely numerous close to the usage of to a venture.

There is one excuse that I pay attention over and over from human beings of every age almost about NOT utilizing to a project, and it has to do with their age. Young people inform me, "Who's going to lease me? I don't have sufficient enjoy, the organization goes to lease a person older with plenty extra capabilities and revel in." Meanwhile older people tell me, "who's going to rent me, I am overqualified, the corporation goes to lease a more youthful individual that has a whole lot of power and brings new mind to the table." The truth is that every fears are unfounded. Age is not some factor more than pretty various. Using your age for not utilising to a activity isn't always some thing greater than an excuse and I say sufficient! Rid your self of these excuses because of the reality they'll be now not doing you any favors.

Just because you are extra youthful or are vintage doesn't advise you aren't going to get the technique. Age isn't a problem while using to a undertaking. I actually have worked with clients of every age that have acquired jobs that they desired due to the truth they have been decided to perform that. They didn't permit age, race, gender or some other problem determine the very last effects and also you shouldn't each. Like I really have said as soon as and I will say it again, jobs do no longer go to people which can be most licensed and characteristic the maximum competencies, jobs visit the person who knows the way to sell themselves, abilties and enjoy to the hiring supervisor. What it comes right all the way down to is self guarantee and advertising and advertising. If you circulate an interview and inspire self belief to the hiring manager and marketplace your abilties, revel in, and understanding, then you stand a first-rate chance of having the undertaking regardless of your age. Therefore, rid yourself of this silly perception that hiring managers obtained't lease due to the fact you're younger or you're antique. If you apprehend that you may do the hobby, then observe.

Most each venture description that I actually have ever glanced at has the subsequent phrase, "exceptional obligations as assigned." People neglect this word and instead attention at the relaxation of the technique description. However, it's miles important for the activity seeker to determine out what the phrase "other obligations as assigned manner" because it may imply the difference amongst you accepting the interest or not taking it. "Other obligations..." also can want to suggest

numerous numerous things and it is as lots as you to decipher the actual because of this within the again of it. The quality time to discover this out is in the route of the interview at the identical time as the hiring supervisor asks, "Do you've got any questions? This is your opportunity to invite. The hiring manager may not give you a concrete answer and truth is that they don't need to. But I can can help you recognize what "other responsibilities as assigned" clearly approach. It means that you will be doing the paintings that nobody else desires to do, the grunt paintings. You can be acting the mind numbing, soul crushing, mundane responsibilities that no individual else wants to do. These are duties that the hiring manager has been geared up to pawn off on any person and that any person is generally the cutting-edge individual. But don't worry due to the fact that's what takes location to most of the fashionable hires. Rest guarantee which you obtained't be doing the ones responsibilities forever however as a minimum for the foreseeable destiny. I sincerely have had to undergo this at every new task that and it's miles continuously a trial. However, being hired as a property supervisor in reality opened my eyes to what "one of a kind obligations as assigned" in reality supposed.

I became hired as a belongings manager for a high town. Initially I turn out to be excited due to the fact I believed that I splendid needed to do walkthroughs of the property that I was assigned. Well, I ultimately observed out that have turn out to be one issue of my assignments. One day my manager called me into her place of work and informed me that I could be doing inspections of housing gadgets. To which I answered,

"I didn't apprehend that I had to research devices."

"It's part of the alternative duties as assigned."

"Okay…. However I even have in no way finished any form of inspections."

"Don't fear approximately it, there's not plenty to it. All you

need to do is look at own family and senior apartments and report deficiencies."

"I see."

My manager ought to tell that I changed into ambivalent approximately the task.

"Listen don't worry, I am pairing you up with Joseph, who's an professional and he's going to train you the entirety you need to apprehend."

"Alright that sounds high-quality" I spoke back. Inspecting gadgets didn't sound hard, ultimately how bad might also moreover want to it's far. I would possibly quick discover. I met with Joseph early the next day.

"Hello there" said Joseph "we may be strolling together, pass in advance and take your pad and pen and ensure you jot down the deficiencies as I factor them out."

"Alright" I responded. "I even have a question."

"Shoot."

"How will I apprehend what a deficiency looks like?"

"Don't fear you'll discover rapid sufficient."

"Okay I am equipped."

"Before we leave make sure you're taking gloves with you."

"Gloves? Why?" I asked

"Trust me."

I ought to quick analyze why I wanted the gloves. However, at that second, I had no idea the disaster zones that I might go to. The first unit had some moderate fixtures out and it become messy but not something out of the regular. However, the second unit opened my eyes to the truth of examining gadgets. We knocked on the door and had been greeted with the resource of a middle-aged female and a repugnant stench and different disgusting odors that I couldn't describe. I desired to cover my nose but stored some distance from doing so due to the reality I didn't need to appear impolite.

"You heady scent that?" asked Joseph.

"Yeah, what is that stench?" seeking out to cover my disgust.

"Infestation."

"What's an infestation?"

But earlier than Joseph can also need to reply, more than one cockroaches scurried past my foot.

"That's an infestation. Be careful in which you step and don't touch some aspect" he replied frivolously and entered. I rapid located on the gloves and entered the condo with hesitation. For those of you that don't understand, an infestation technique the presence of insects and animals and in this example, it supposed cockroaches and mice.

As quick as we entered, I positioned mice droppings on the ground and cockroaches crawling everywhere within the cabinets. I assumed that it modified into due to the overflowing trash within the kitchen that spilled out onto the floor.

"Excuse me, even as can the exterminator stop via to address roach and mice hassle?" asked the tenant.

"Well ma'am, eliminating your trash will do away with that pest hassle" responded Joseph.

"I don't count on so" she answered as she walked beyond the trash heap.

I shook my head in disbelief. As we endured walking through the unit, I determined deficiency upon deficiency. Light fixtures were now not operating, electric powered powered shops had missing cowl plates, and a smog detector modified into eliminated from the living room.

"What took place to the smoke detector?" requested Joseph.

"There became no smoke detector as soon as I moved in" answered the tenant.

"Ma'am please, all gadgets embody the smoke detectors."

"Alright! Alright! I took it off because it became making the ones loud noises that didn't permit me sleep." She went into the drawer and pulls out a mangled smoke detector and passed it over.

"What came about to this?" I asked.

"I tried to repair it with a hammer."

"Fix it! It looks as if you smashed it more than one times" replied Joseph.

"Damn detail wouldn't save you making noise."

"Ma'am we're going to invoice you for this" stated Joseph.

"I don't understand why, it nonetheless works."

We didn't say something and continued with the inspection and I persevered writing down the deficiencies. In addition to this, I had to observe in which I stepped due to the truth there were mice droppings anywhere. Afterwards I changed into relieved to be out of there however that became certainly the start. I had fifty distinct gadgets to have a look at and loads of them had been just as terrible as the second one unit. Afterwards, I once more to my administrative center and feature come to be satisfied that I didn't need to do inspections of gadgets to any amount in addition. Moments later, the supervisor called me into her workplace.

"How did it pass?"

I didn't reply, I modified into harassed.

"That awful, huh? Well, try to placed at the present time behind you but you continue to want to check out more gadgets."

"How many extra?" I asked.

"About a hundred and fifty."

My jaw dropped.

"Listen, I can't get actually all of us else to try this, so that you will need to do it for now."

"I apprehend." I sighed because of the fact I knew that I had no preference. I had signed up for the pastime and now changed into caught with this project. I had no manner out. I did inspections for eight months and the manager in the end took mercy on me and exceeded the challenge to the newly hired assets supervisor and I even have come to be glad whilst she did. Now every time I start a modern-day-day hobby, I make certain to invite what "specific responsibilities as assigned" method.

Temporary and element-time jobs are a course into a whole-time technique.

When searching out employment, you may probably have your points of interest set on getting a entire-time task with blessings at a exceptional business enterprise. However, all you're finding is part-time or temporary positions. The truth is that complete-time jobs are difficult to achieve because of the truth the opposition is fierce. Especially if it's miles a nicely-paying assignment with advantages. That's why it's far critical to keep an open thoughts and remember element-time and/or brief employment. The cause being that the ones positions can also additionally furthermore ultimately come to be complete-time positions in the end. Let's say that you hired for a transient position and 3 months later it ends and also you don't get hired on. Even in case you don't get hired on at least you gain new abilties and can upload that, at the thing of the revel in, on your resume and this could result in many greater opportunities.

The truth approximately the phrase "favored" that looks on undertaking postings.

The word preferred seems on many system descriptions. You will come upon it within the revel in and education component of the technique description. For example,

"bachelor's degree- preferred"

"Two years of virtual marketing- desired."

The phrase "preferred" discourages candidates from utilizing to severa jobs. The cause is that they accept as true with that simplest human beings that meet those particular qualifications should comply with. But that's a false impression. The truth is that "preferred" in truth method that when you have the ones positive qualifications, that's wonderful however if you don't have it, it's no longer a large deal. Like I genuinely have usually said if you could do 30% of the process then you definitely have to exercise as it method that you have the fundamental knowledge of the interest and the relaxation you may take a look at at the pastime. Now in case you see the word "required" that is unique. For example:

Nurse Assistant certification required.

When the phrase required seems on a undertaking description it approach which you want to have the talent or the certification and there's no manner spherical this. Most vocational trades which encompass welder, dental assistant, and vocational nurse require that you be certified in advance than they may rent you. Once once more at the same time as you spot the word "desired" and you are assured that you can do the process, then move in advance and examine.

I communicate from revel in due to the fact I even have applied to severa jobs in which I had minimal experience however yet I become provided the region. The purpose that I get gadget offers is due to the fact I pass into the interview with the most self belief and persuade the hiring manager that I am the nice candidate for the placement. Am I sincerely the pleasant candidate? I don

't recognize because of the fact I never meet the opportunity applicants but I don't ought to meet them to recognize that I can do the assignment. And the fact is that the hiring supervisor will simplest simply recognize that I can do the hobby as soon as I get hired on. Therefore, if you revel in you can do the machine, then exercise and pass into the interview with self guarantee and convince the hiring manger that you are the excellent candidate.

Chapter 2: Employment Groups Are Unique

Employment organizations have professionals and cons and I will not honestly knock on them due to the fact I be given as genuine with that they do serve a cause. But it's far critical for process seekers to apprehend the fact about how they feature. First off employment businesses artwork at once with employers. Second there are numerous kinds of companies that cater to particular task sectors together with workplace, manufacturing, warehouse, and so on.... Third, employment businesses paintings speedy and place a challenge seeker at a piece internet site proper away. You can show as much as a venture company in recent times and you can have a mission the very next day. This is outstanding in particular in case you are in dire want of a paycheck. These are the extremely good factors of the use of a staffing business enterprise. However, there are poor elements which you want to recognize if you decide to use them. The major rule of employment companies is that while you receives a commission, they gets a fee. They can take anywhere from five to 15 percent of your paycheck. That's why it's far of their terrific interest to location you at a bit net website online as fast as viable. In addition to this, most corporations will region you at a quick feature with a view to sooner or later end. When the brief job ends, then the interest seeker will go back to the company and the sample maintains and the economic organisation organisation keeps to gets a charge. It is not inside the organization's excellent interest for a task seeker to accumulate complete-time everlasting employment because of the fact then they lose their golden goose. Once over again employment businesses do serve a motive and there are experts to using them, but it's miles vital to consider that they stand to take benefit of you. In addition to employment companies, there are personnel improvement companies that function within the identical fashion. However the fundamental distinction is that they do no longer price for his or her enterprise and offer various belongings and device for people seeking out employment.

Interviews

The cause that interviews are nerve wracking for pastime seekers is because of the truth they'll be not certain what to anticipate, what to mention, and a manner to behave. In addition to this most manner seekers suppose that via the usage of answering the interview questions efficiently, it'll possibly be sufficient to get the machine. However, this is an extended way from the fact. The interview questions are an essential element of the interview, but they may be no longer the give up-all. There are other elements that hiring managers reflect onconsideration on while offering a method to an character. For instance, they think about an applicant's bodily look and demeanor in addition to their response to high-quality questions. For this segment, I interest at the lesser-recognized elements of the interview collectively with the length of interviews, the cause which you get invited to an interview, and the cruel fact of interviewing it simply is, you're being judged in the direction of your interview.

It is crucial to take into account that masses of humans observe to at least one function. Especially if that feature pays properly and gives great benefits. It is likewise essential to take into account that if you get referred to as in for an interview, you then are a part of the small percentage that handed the primary segment of the interview. This approach that your nicely-written resume stuck the attention of the hiring manager. Now it's as a whole lot as you to capitalize on the state of affairs. The first thing you must do is decide out what unique skills or enjoy stuck the hiring manager's hobby. You can determine this out while the hiring manager says "Tell me about yourself." First, introduce yourself, talk approximately your maximum precious capabilities. Second speak approximately your revel in. If you do that right, the hiring manager will study up with a question about a selected skills which you referred to For instance, they might say "You mentioned digital advertising, are you able to please inform me more about that?" When a hiring supervisor asks a observe up question, it way which you piqued their interest and you need to capitalize at the scenario. Now if this doesn't arise, you continue to have some different opportunity. During the interview, whilst the hiring supervisor asks you, "Do you have got any questions?" Then you could ask. "What abilties or enjoy stood out on my resume? Most instances they may be honest and could will will let you recognize and after they do you may follow up and popularity on that unique expertise or experience. The whole aspect right right right here is to factor out your extraordinary attributes. By doing this, you considerably beautify your probabilities of getting the venture.

Research the organisation and the hiring manager earlier than your interview.

In this factor in time of the net, something and the whole thing can be seemed up. When it includes interviewing, it's miles critical which you do your due diligence and look up the enterprise that you will be working for. Learn their assignment declaration and values, get to apprehend the products and services they provide, parent out what they may be trying to accomplish and how you could help them out. In addition to all this, moreover look up the hiring supervisor and take a look at extra approximately them due to the reality this may provide you with a bonus you need. Let me provide an explanation for.

When you get a call for an interview, the man or woman putting the appointment will let you know who you will be interviewing with. Now, with this statistics, do your due diligence and look up the individual. By doing this, you may take a look at plenty about the individual at the side of their accomplishments, initiatives that they are involved in, subjects that they will be enthusiastic about. Use this facts in your benefit. For example, allow's say that you have an interview with Mr. Smith from ABC organisation employer and also you look him up if you want to examine him. While doing all of your studies, you research that similarly to being the hiring supervisor, Mr. Smith volunteers at his kids's university and at his church.

So now you recognize that volunteering is crucial for him. Therefore, if you have ever volunteer or are currently volunteering, you can deliver this as a incredible deal as his hobby and curry pick with him. Whatever statistics you take a look at, use it on your benefit. Maybe each of you attended the same college or have the equal hobbies and pastimes. Whatever the case can be the critical aspect is to set up a reference to the person that may be interviewing you. If you experience that searching up the hiring supervisor is regular, truly don't forget that the hiring manager maximum in all likelihood will look you up. Therefore, do now not sense bad in case you look up the hiring manager or the organisation. It is to your great interest to observe and recognize who exactly you'll be working for and with.

Schedule one interview consistent with day.

One of the largest mistakes that a activity seeker can do is to time desk two or greater interviews in the equal day. You could likely ask your self why is that a mistake? After all I am being proactive and improving my chances of touchdown a procedure. To a sure diploma that is correct but the fact is that via scheduling interviews in in a few unspecified time inside the future, you're doing greater harm than top. Let me offer an reason behind.

First off, in case you are interviewing for a well-paying challenge with outstanding blessings, anticipate the interview to closing 40 mins to an hour or perhaps longer. Second, some interviews consist, no longer best of panel interviews, but spherical of interviews all inside the identical day. The fact is that you could never recognize how prolonged or excessive your interview may be, consequently it's far on your first-class interest to time table one interview in step with day. In addition to this, you need to moreover deliver your self sufficient time to mirror at the interview itself. You want to reflect onconsideration on the questions that have been requested and the responses that you gave. Maybe you have been asked a question that you had in no way been asked in advance than or maybe some component occurred at some point of the interview that left you flustered. Whatever the case perhaps, you need to offer your self time to step lower lower back, mirror or even vent. Every interview can be particular and no interviews can be alike. I understand that some humans can be in rush to acquire a mission and consequently squeeze or three interviews consistent with day. But pretty frankly you're doing yourself a disservice. At that frantic pace you can burn your self out and now not supply your terrific to each interview.

That's why I extraordinarily recommend to spread out your interviews and do one constant with day and I speak from a personal experience that had me reeling for days.

I had an interview with a prestigious college. I became excited and irritating but I modified into organized, I had carried out my due diligence and researched each the college and the hiring manager. I have end up prepared every in mind and frame. Before the interview began, I took a deep breath and composed myself. The interview commenced and I turn out to be ready to talk about myself due to the truth I knew for a fact that most interviews started out with the vintage "Tell me approximately your self." However this time, the interview didn't begin like with that query. Instead, the hiring manager started the interview with, "Do you've got were given any questions for me?" I modified into surprised due to the truth I had no longer anticipated that question at that 2nd, that query is normally asked on the cease of the interview. Therefore, whilst she asked me that question, it threw me for a loop. My thoughts went clean, no question got here to thoughts, and the purpose that for this become due to the fact I expected that query in the direction of the give up. I in the end requested a query but to at the prevailing time, I can't don't forget what I requested. For the rest of the interview, I become discombobulated. After 40 minutes, the interview ended and I became not happy with the results. Afterwards, I vented to my friend Susan.

"How should she start with that question? You don't begin interviews with that question."

"But she did."

"I apprehend she did but it's a for the reason that that precise query comes inside the direction of the cease of the interview."

"Don't fear an excessive amount of approximately it. How do you revel in about the rest of the interview?"

"It turns out to be ok however that rattling query!"

"Get over it. It's finished, there's not something you may do about it."

Susan have come to be proper, there was no longer tons I can also need to do approximately it. However it stayed with me for more than one days. I didn't get the location but that didn't trouble me. What did trouble me changed into that I need to have been organized for anything, as a good buy as and which encompass that question. But chalk it as much as revel in.

Chapter 3: The Course Of The Interview

When you visit an interview, you are being judged. Some people can also argue and say that's wrong or unfair however it has no longer something to do with the ones subjects, the merciless fact is which you are being judged, from your appearance, to what you are saying and which includes what you don't say. The first element which you are being choose on, is your appearance and demeanor. Do you appearance presentable? Are you exceptional and feature a fantastic individual? You may also ask, properly why must a hiring supervisor decide me on my persona? They do it due to the reality the person who is hired can be a consultant of the employer. Therefore, the person that is hired want to appearance presentable, brilliant, and professional continually.

In addition to that, everything you do in advance than, throughout, and after the interview is likewise being judged. A false impression that many activity seekers have, is that an interview starts offevolved the moment that they begin to answer the interview questions. The truth is that the interview begins offevolved within the intervening time you enter the lobby. From that second, the entirety you're pronouncing and the whole thing that you do is being judged. If you are making small communicate with the receptionist, if you take out your telephone and scroll, the way which you deliver yourself, your body language, facial features, all that is being taken into consideration. That is why it's far critical to be for your pleasant conduct in a few unspecified time within the future of the entire interview way. Hiring managers are continuously searching out any red flags with a view to disqualify you for the location. How do I understand this? Because on every occasion that I clearly have interviewed humans, I be aware about their appearance, demeanor, and personality. I be aware of their body language as it speaks extent. I comprehend that I am no longer the most effective one to do that due to the fact, this has been completed to me as properly.

I as fast as had an interview for a library manager characteristic and believed that I have become a shoo-in for the place mainly due to the fact I had the experience, skills, and statistics. Due to this, I didn't problem dressing up for the interview. Instead, I confirmed as an awful lot as the interview in a polo shirt, denims, and tennis shoes. In my defense, they have been great tennis shoes. I knew that I become underdressed once I observed the relaxation of the opportunity candidates, they all wore enterprise employer garb and regarded expert and there I have become with my polo shirt, denims, and pleasant tennis footwear. But it didn't hassle me. I patiently waited my flip and whilst my call turn out to be referred to as, I had been given up and made my manner to the interview room. I believed that I have become going to be interviewed through a low-rating member of the library however I come to be incorrect.

"Hi I am Samantha Roberts, Director for ABC Library." That's right! I changed into going to be interviewed with the useful resource of the top honcho of the library. While introducing herself she looked at me and had this disapproving appearance that screamed, "You do recognize that that is an interview, proper?" But her harsh look didn't faze me the least bit. I have become clearly assured. I need to experience that she have become reluctant to interview me based on my look. She started out asking the questions with a scowl on her face and her fingers crossed but even this didn't deter me. She pitched interview query after interview question and I knocked every taken into consideration one in every of them out of the ballpark. As the interview persevered, her scowl morphed into a grin and her arms uncrossed. By the time the interview had concluded, I had won her over with my resounding solutions, self belief, and exuberance. One week later, I have been given the decision and modified into provided the library position.

It's ok to mention that you had been fired from your previous feature sooner or later of the interview.

Being fired from a process is the maximum disturbing aspect which could seem to every body. Many people take a long time to recover from being fired or maybe when they get higher, they do now not a way to circulate earlier. They recognize they want to get each distinctive interest but they may be no longer positive within the event that they've to carry up that they have been fired at a few stage within the interview. And within the event that they do deliver it up, how do they tell this to the hiring supervisor without looking terrible? It's now not clean. But there may be a way to say this sensitive issue remember.

The first element to realize is that there can be existence after being fired and you may get a brand new mission even if you have been fired from your preceding one. I say this with the maximum confidence because I have been fired on numerous activities from super jobs and feature recovered and effectively received new employment. The second problem to bear in mind is to be sincere about getting fired.

Hiring managers will not hold in opposition to you. But the caveat right right here is to be sincere about what came about. Truth is that almost all of human beings have been fired from a venture. Hiring managers are human and recognize that firings do rise up and a number of them are inclined to present you a 2d danger. Therefore, be sincere with them and inform them which you were fired and that, you aren't the equal individual you as quickly as had been. You found out of your errors, you have got got had been given matured and you're organized to make contributions to the well-being of the enterprise agency. The hiring manager might be stimulated collectively along with your honesty and may moreover be inspired with, the way you have become your existence round. How do I understand this? Because I became fired and arrested from my first mission.

The first technique I had become at 18 years vintage, at a well-known track save that bought information and compact discs. It have become a dream come proper due to the reality I cherished song and the idea of listening to music while running changed into great. The first few weeks have been brilliant and I loved it. But then I did some component truely silly and changed into fired and arrested at the same time. The keep had this ordinary wherein they opened a compact disc and played it on the shop's stereo. Afterwards they might located it away in a drawer and in the end discard it at the identical time as it got carefully broken.

I had been given this stupid idea that no person should miss it, if I took one opened disc. So I did it and no character determined. After that I have become brazen and took some other after which a few one-of-a-kind and a few different. Now the shops had cameras but that didn't deter me from stealing the discs. Well enough to mention that one morning I have become referred to as into the supervisor's administrative center, she showed me the surveillance images that confirmed that I took the disc. Shortly thereafter, I became fired and arrested instantaneous. Due to this I acquired a misdemeanor that is however on my document. There modified into no way to cowl this misdemeanor especially even as it got here to utilizing for jobs. Therefore, I had no exceptional desire but to be honest about the incident particularly every time I crammed out a system software or had an interview. I knew that the organization might also want to look at, ultimately, approximately the misdemeanor, therefore I grow to be in advance approximately it. Now the manner I went about mentioning this incident inside the direction of the interview become in a clever way. Toward the surrender of the interview, the hiring managers asked me, if there has been a few factor else that I wanted to percentage and my response have grow to be continuously positive and that is the reaction I gave.

I want to will permit you to realise that I actually have a misdemeanor on my report because of a petty robbery that I dedicated when I emerge as greater youthful. I made a massive mistake and I am not the same man or woman as earlier than. I positioned out from my mistakes and observe the mistake of my strategies. If given this possibility, I realize that I might be grateful and could be an honest worker. I could apprehend if you will don't forget me for this characteristic and I manner to your time.

I gave this same speech on every occasion I had an interview for at the least ten years at once. And it worked due to the reality I changed into furnished process after hobby. After ten years, I stopped mentioning the misdemeanor but I comprehend that if it ever gets added up in a few unspecified time inside the future of the interviews, I need to be sincere approximately this episode in my existence.

Your interviews can be long…in truth long.

The hiring manager calls you for an interview and you accept. You expect that the interview must not be prolonged and that you may be finished with the interview inner an less luxurious time. The fact is that interviews can closing a long time, in particular if it is a nicely-paying project. If the pay is $25 and over, assume to be in that interview for over 40 mins to an hour and now and again longer. Furthermore, expect to be interviewed by means of way of a couple of human beings. Sometimes it can be a panel interview and from time to time it's far spherical of interviews in that same day. The truth is that you'll not recognize how prolonged an interview can be because of the reality the hiring manager will not allow you to realize and they don't want to. That's why it is essential that you be organized. Make certain you're taking pen and paper to write down down notes and take water with you. Yes! Water. After being apprehensive and speaking for additonal than thirty mins, your throat may be parched and you may have a difficult time answering questions. I were on many lengthy interviews and they were all particular. However I want to tell you about a particular interview that I went to that just went on and on and modified right into a waste of time however an outstanding analyzing experience.

I grow to be invited to interview for a network college. I grow to be to meet with Mrs. Palermo at three:30pm. Of route, I had been given there early because of the fact I wanted to appear professional. I made my way to the reception desk and informed the receptionist that I turn out to be there to look Ms. Palermo. The receptionist stated tremendous she's looking forward to you.

"Please follow me." I became organized to meet and provoke her with my interview abilities however I modified into incorrect and that is the instantaneous at the same time as the ordeal began. The receptionist led me to a pc lab and stated, "The first phase of the interview is that you want to take a a couple of-desire exam which encompass 50 questions and you have 15 minutes to reply the questions. Don't rush via the examination due to the truth wrong solutions will don't forget within the direction of you however try to complete the venture." I smiled and nodded. I completed that vain more than one-preference examination and turned into happy to attain this. Afterwards the receptionist made a cellular smartphone call which I figured have become so I ought to meet with Ms. Palermo. I sat and waited and mins later I changed into greeted with the useful resource of the usage of a tall, husky, male which I assumed wasn't Ms. Palermo. "Hello Mr. Gabriel, thank you for coming in in recent times. My call is Robert and I may be guiding you via the second one segment of the interview." It changed into then that I knew that I end up in for an extended, hard interview technique however I smiled and nodded. "Mr. Gabriel, on this second segment you may be interviewed on my own and three of my other colleagues." Great I idea to myself however I knew that this modified into part of the approach so I went alongside. It modified into the essential panel interview with the same old solid of characters. There become the outgoing, jolly individual, the bored and irritated individual, the blunt and clean individual, and the quiet one that didn't say a few element however saved looking at me. I had achieved many panel interviews in my lifetime so none of these people intimidated me. They asked the standard interview questions and I knocked every one in each of them out of the ballpark. Finally, after 40 minutes, they congratulated for a great interview session. "Well Mr. Gabriel" stated Robert, "we would like that allows you to circulate straight away to the following a part of the interview method." Finally, I am going to fulfill Ms. Palermo, I idea to myself. I became incorrect. "We want you to fulfill with the university president so he have to provide you with a historical past at the college." I smiled and nodded and sighed quietly. I met the college president and in choice to him telling me the history of the college, he suggested me all about his accomplishments and didn't request from me one single interview query. He in the long run stopped after 15 minutes and informed me that I would possibly meet with Ms. Palermo. After what regarded like an eternity, (in reality one hour and twenty minutes) I met with Ms. Palermo and through the use of the use of then I had no desire to artwork for that ridiculous college. However, I am professional so I endured with the interview manner and answered the identical interview questions that the panel had already asked. I without a doubt puzzled why Ms. Palermo couldn't were part of the panel interview so I wouldn't have lengthy long past through this ordeal all all over again. After one hour and forty-five minutes, I come to be launched with out a indication in the occasion that they may offer me the process. Just the fact that I had prolonged past through that ridiculous ordeal, I need to had been provided the system without delay. But exact day I don't make the pointers. So I left and I never obtained a cellphone call from that university and I thank god that I by no means had to bypass lower returned to that so known as "better-reading organization."

Panel interviews are tough but now not not possible to pull off.

Panel interviews are the hardest interviews to drag off particularly due to the fact you're being interviewed thru 2 or extra people. It is probably four, 6, or greater human beings and the hardest thing is that you need to provoke all participants of the panels. If you fail to hook up with even considered sincerely one in all them, you can not get the machine. The key to pulling off the panel interview is to be genuinely confident, enthusiastic, and now not be intimidated with the useful aid of the panel individuals. I say this due to the fact each person inside the panel interview has a position to play. For example, you have got the lively man or woman, this character is glad and giddy with satisfaction approximately the interview. Then you have got the direct individual that comes across as brazen and rude. There's also the distracted person that looks as if they would as an alternative be somewhere else and the listing of members goes on and on. The cause they do this is because of the truth they'll be seeking to look the manner you react to each man or woman. After all you'll be interacting with the ones personalities each day, therefore it's far in their top notch hobby to lease the right character with the proper persona. Here some hints that I can percent with you. When answering a query, cope with the person that requested the query and broadly recognized the rest of the institution via technique of creating eye touch with all of them. Also supply lots of copies of your resume. Imagine if you show up to an interview with two copies of your resume however there are 4 humans inside the panel interview, how do you observed that makes you appearance? Also ensure which you have interaction with all the panel people, do no longer supply all of your attention to at least one sole person. Finally make sure to stay enthusiastic at some point of the tool. In my expert existence, I absolutely have had my sincere percent of panel interviews and in spite of the fact that some of them were daunting, they're terrific studying reports.

The biggest panel interview that I did, consisted of 8 people. That's proper eight human beings for one method. I knew that I even have become going to do a panel however upon entering the room I walked proper right into a room with an extended table and sitting throughout the desk there had been 8 people. Some of them appeared happy, multiple them bored, others indifferent and one seemed like he changed into prepared to doze off. I replied the inquiries to the awesome of my capacity. I extensively identified all and sundry inside the room and I remained confident at a few stage within the interview. Unfortunately, I actually have become not decided on for the place but I come to be happy that I had lengthy past via with it as it gave me the possibility to exercise no longer most effective the solutions however additionally the shipping, it definitely is simply as essential.

Even though I even have emerge as not a achievement in that panel interview, I have been successful in one-of-a-kind panel interviews. For example, once I interviewed for a Library Manager characteristic, the panel consisted of three people. When I interviewed for a Marketing Associate, the panel consisted of four humans. When I interviewed for the Trainer characteristic, the panel consisted of three people. I correctly handed every of these panel interviews and changed into furnished the manner. The reality is that despite the fact that interviewing does not make me fearful, I despite the fact that need to positioned in the paintings and make sure I blow away the opposition in case you want to land the activity.

Chapter 4: Revealing Truths Approximately

When answering interview questions, you're strolling a first rate line amongst saying sufficient but now not revealing too much approximately yourself. An interview is nerve racking and at the same time as someone is concerned, they each generally have a propensity to clam up or speak too much. If you clam up, you then definately aren't capable to tell the hiring supervisor all about your splendid talents, experience, and knowledge. And if you are the opportunity and speak too much, then you may emerge as speakme about your non-public life, issues, and awesome beside the factor topics. So, what's a project seeker to do? Well you need to speak at some point of the interview however even as you do make certain that every one your responses are process related. Now in this segment of the e-book, I help you answer positive interview question but additionally provide a brief heritage on information on the query. Remember that each interview questions is being asked for a specific purpose. The hiring supervisor is making an attempt to advantage belief about you, your person, your paintings ethic.

The greater they find out about you, the better they're capable of render a desire whether or not or no longer or not to lease you or no longer. Do I cover all the interview questions, I do not. But I do move over the most crucial ones which can be important to your interview. The solutions that I offer aren't a one period fits all, that means that no longer every body can use those solutions. But I offer an cause for the way you may solution and provide specific examples. Let's get started out.

"What is your weak spot?"

Most humans dread answering this query due to the fact they don't want to be seen in a terrible slight. Therefore, they solution it incorrectly or make up a few lame reaction. For example, they'll say. "My weak point is that I am a perfectionist…" This is a cop out answer which means that that you are heading off answering the question altogether. The fact is that no individual is a perfectionist due to the truth no longer some thing ever comes out ideal. The purpose human beings use this situation is due to the fact this answer doesn't depict them in a negative mild. Now even as answering this query, you need to provide an sincere answer. Hiring managers ask you this query, now not due to the fact they want to understand your susceptible factor however they need to apprehend what you're doing approximately your susceptible issue. Are you being proactive? There are many ways to reply this query and I will provide examples. When answering the question, you could provide a professional or personal susceptible point. I will begin with a professional susceptible point.

I discovered that inside the hobby description it states that one need to be proficient at excel. I can in truth say that I definitely have limited knowledge on excel. However, I am taking up-line classes, looking tutorials, and analyzing books and I am tremendous that it's simplest a rely of time earlier than I turn out to be proficient at excel. I am talented at different software program which encompass phrase, electricity detail, adobe, consequently I are privy to it's great a rely wide variety of time before I am an professional at excel.

First off, word how I didn't factor out the phrase weak point in my answer. Second, I didn't say, I didn't recognize anything approximately excel, I said I actually have limited know-how. Third, I stated the measures that I am taking to fight this weak spot. That's what hiring managers need to listen, they need to concentrate how you are being proactive approximately your weak point. Now if that's a professional weakness, here is a personal weak spot.

A weak spot of mine is that I am shy around new humans. I have a propensity to be quiet and aloof and honestly say enough clearly so humans apprehend I am present. However, almost approximately paintings, my shyness isn't always an obstacle. At paintings, I exit of my manner to introduce myself to all of us and permit them to comprehend who I am and what I do due to the reality I comprehend that teamwork might be very critical inside the administrative center. I additionally am the primary to volunteer for brand spanking new sports or committees, consequently I understand that my shyness will now not be an trouble in the place of job.

In the instance above, I reassured the hiring supervisor that my weak point will not be a element and that I am proactive via going out of my manner and interact with my coworkers. Whichever way you make a decision to answer the susceptible element query, non-public or expert, actually make sure which you u.S.A. The measures which you are taking to triumph over your weak point.

Now if you are not certain what weakness to talk about, I truely have an answer for you. All, if now not most hobby descriptions, listing the exquisite skills that they choice to appearance in their new worker. Look thru that listing and pick a talent or which you are not talented at, on the way to be your prone factor. Once you have decided at the susceptible factor, then decide out what measures you're taking to show that weakness right into a power. You can try this with any task description.

Describing difficult conditions inside the place of work.

Tell me approximately a task which you faced on your previous administrative center and the way did you overcome it?

Tell me approximately a time in that you disagreed with a coworker and the way did you remedy it?

When it involves answering those questions, the important element to hold in thoughts is to maintain your answers at the mild thing. Do now not speak about dramatic sports that passed off at work. Refrain from talking approximately arguments, squabbles, or conflicts that had been given out of manage. Especially don't convey up a struggle that escalated in which your supervisor had to get worried. These kinds of incidents make you appearance unprofessional and unreliable, even if it isn't your fault. Therefore, even as you answer these questions make certain which you keep your responses at the moderate detail. Talk about a hassle that didn't cause an excessive amount of friction and which you have been able to remedy. For example, you could say;

I changed into working in an place of business and I overheard Sam answer the telephone in an unprofessional manner. After the choice, I took him apart and informed him that he couldn't solution the cellphone in any such manner. He disagreed and believed that he might also need to. I explained cellphone etiquette and system and techniques. I informed him that I actually have grow to be fine looking for for his and the commercial enterprise employer's awesome hobby. He understood and from that 2nd on, he answered the cellphone in a well mannered and accurate manner.

Notice how the war wasn't severe, it wasn't dramatic and greater importantly I treated the scenario and didn't get the supervisor involved. The fact is that hiring managers don't want to pay hobby number one troubles. They have already got enough troubles as it is and if you sound as even though you would probably create troubles for them, then it'll put you out of the walking for the region. Therefore, I intently endorse staying a long way from the heavy stuff.

"What is your earnings requirement?"

This is a few other query that procedure seekers do now not like to reply due to the reality they don't apprehend the way to answer it. Should they ask for the minimum? Is it adequate to transport past the profits range? Also how do you declare how an awful lot you want to get paid without sounding determined or worrying? Before I answer those questions, it's miles essential which you understand your definitely well worth. You want to realise how a exquisite deal you need to receives a fee and can't deviate from it. Think approximately the minimum amount that YOU are willing to take, now not the minimal that the agency desires to pay you. It is essential which you have a figure in thoughts due to the fact fact is that the organisation is searching for to pay you the minimal or perhaps a top notch deal a lot much less as it saves the organization coins. That's why it is essential that you have a determine in thoughts. Let's say for instance, which you provide you with a determine that is $22 an hour. Now bump it up three figures and you've got a selection, $22-$25 hour. However, it is not enough which you claim how a whole lot you're seeking to receives a commission. You need to moreover provide an reason behind why the employer goes to pay you that an awful lot. For instance;

I am looking for to make amongst $22-$25 an hour because of my abilties and revel in. I am certain that I very personal valuable capabilities which encompass advertising and advertising and public presentation which could help your corporation boom. In addition to that, I am additionally a collection participant, tech savvy, and bilingual in languages.

By advertising and marketing and advertising your capabilities, you are justifying the cause that the agency is going to pay you what you are inquiring for. Now at the same time as you answer, you need to reap this with self notion and assertiveness. If you are missing self perception or aren't high-quality a way to enhance yourself assure, you could pick up my e-book,

Sell, promote, sell How to Land Your Dream Job by using Marketing your Skills, Experience, and Knowledge and so you can train you a way to boost yourself notion and marketplace yourself to the corporation.

As a long way as going outside the profits range, you may do so. You can ask for added than what is stated on the interest posting. Let's bypass lower lower back to the example of $22-$25 consistent with hour. There is not any rule that says which you must stay inside this range. You can ask for delivered and you must ask in case you experience that you are really well worth it. You might be amazed at how many hiring managers will provide you with what you need, in case you most effective ask. The trouble is that humans are afraid to ask due to the fact they agree with that in the event that they gain this they'll not be taken into consideration for the area. That is a opportunity however in case you recognise your well really worth then you definately absolutely want to claim it. I virtually have worked with many clients which can be too shy to ask for what they want and so they take the technique at a pay that they are not happy with but they accept as true with that they have to be thrilled approximately the assignment. I disagree with this belief. If you accept as true with which you are simply well worth a certain quantity then declare it and allow the chips fall in which they will. That's self belief.

Tell me something personal approximately yourself. (Should I truly communicate approximately my personal lifestyles?)

First off whilst answering this question, chorus from speaking about your personal existence. The purpose being is that some thing non-public data you put reachable, the hiring supervisor can maintain it in opposition to you. Is this truthful? Of direction now not. But does it seem? Of path, it does. For instance, you would in all likelihood say that you enjoy gambling on line video video games. Now within the hiring supervisor's eyes, you appear immature and no longer organized for duties due to the truth you enjoy playing video video video games. Even if you do enjoy playing on-line video video games, do now not be sincere. Be selective about what you're going to tell the hiring manager. So, proper right right here's the give up whilst answering the question, speak about your private life because it pertains to paintings.

This basically approach that you tie on your non-public activities in your expert lifestyles. Let's say which you enjoy exercise which includes lifting weights, trekking, swimming, and so on.. So now you tie in exercise into your expert existence and your answer may sound like this.

On my day off, I revel in hiking and the usage of my motorcycle. I do those sports because it allows me loosen up and clear my mind. Then when I go back to work I accumulate this in a non violent nation of thoughts and may address my duties in an inexperienced way.

You can follow any amusement hobby to this reaction which consist of analyzing, gambling an device, or volunteering. The whole factor is that some thing interest you do to your day without work, it allows you be a green character at art work.

Hiring managers are not allowed to invite sure questions.

In case you didn't comprehend, there are certain questions that hiring managers are not allowed to invite. They can't ask you questions about the following subjects;

Sex

Gender

Marital Status

Race

Age

Ethnicity

You are blanketed via the law and do no longer want to answer. If a hiring manager does supply up any such topics, you can with courtesy decline to answer. If they're insistent then you may terminate the interview with the aid of virtually responding inside the following manner, "I do now not need to answer the query and do now not desire to keep with the interview." You are included with the beneficial resource of the law and in addition to this the hiring managers realize that they're able to get in problem through asking those unique questions.

Chapter 5: Trick Interview Questions

Every so frequently a hiring supervisor will throw a curveball question moreover called a "difficult" query If you think that an interview query is hard to answer, then a flowery interview query is lots greater hard. The purpose that the ones questions are asked is to have a have a look at and gauge your response. There are applicants that becomes flustered and beaten thru tough questions. Then there are those people as a manner to upward push above it all and could answer them in a diligent and efficient way. It is vital to keep in mind at the same time as answering those "complicated questions" to live calm and not lose your cool due to the fact in case you do, it might positioned you out of the on foot for the location. I will cover "complicated" questions that I honestly have dealt with. In my opinion the subsequent questions are tough to answer as it's basically a lure, that during case you are not careful, you could fall into. The first trick query isn't always a query however a assertion however it's miles impactful.

You have a outstanding resume with awesome abilities and experience, however I just don't think that you can do the activity.

Upon being attentive to this, an applicant may additionally moreover lose their composure and may fit off on the hiring manager. But you acquired't try this, due to the fact you understand better than that. I will let you know a way to react, a manner to respond, and a way to have a look at up. First off you could stay calm and steadfast. Before answering take a second to take a breath, accumulate your mind, and respond.

I understand which you have your doubts however I can guarantee that I can do the pastime if given the possibility. In my preceding function I met and passed all my desires. Furthermore, my competencies and large experience align with the enterprise's dreams. If given the possibility, I realize that I can excel due to the fact I truly have performed this for the preceding corporations that I simply have worked at. If you have got each other questions or if there can be a few component which you need me to make clear on my resume, I may be satisfied to gain this.

Not great did you assure the hiring supervisor that you can do the method however you informed him that you may assist the corporation, all the in the period in-between offering great provider. Hiring managers want to pay interest this, they need to be reassured which you have what it takes to do the task and that you won't be disenchanted via manner of terms that don't imply a lot.

Tell me about a time that you failed on your expert profession and the way did you conquer it?

In my ebook, Sell, Sell, Sell. I u . S . That it's far essential that a manner seeker refrain from pronouncing horrible terms which includes can't, received't, don't comprehend, and so on.... at some level within the interview. The purpose is if you say sufficient terrible phrases, then you definitely definately obtained't get the challenge. The word fail is a poor word consequently while you reply to this question, you want to abstain from saying I failed whilst...By mentioning this you are admitting defeat and also you shouldn't. The most effective time that you fail in lifestyles is at the same time as you actually give up and lay down. But I recognize that most human beings are resilient and will fight for what they want. Therefore you are a fighter and now not a failure. So how do you answer this question without pronouncing the phrase failed. Think of a word this is nearly like failure however a good deal much less intense, as an instance the phrase setback. This word way which you had been met with boundaries but you overcame those barriers. Now permit's use the word setback in choice to failure.

I haven't had a professional failure as a good buy as I had setbacks in my expert career. In my current-day function as a presenter, I did virtual presentations to the overall public. Initially I became unusual with this layout, I made errors and had setbacks however I didn't surrender. I changed into persistent and learned the manner to do virtual presentations. Now, I can do each in character and virtual indicates.

The trick right here isn't to admit that you failed. Instead, you had setbacks in your expert profession but you determined out from them and matured and evolved. These are genuinely examples of "tough" interview questions. There is severa those form of questions. The thriller is not to get beaten through using them and approach to the high-quality of your capability.

I will go away you with one final tip about interviewing. With most of these interviews, you need to be prepared to reply any question with out fear, hesitation, or trepidation. Furthermore, you have to be organized to improvise instantaneous due to the reality the hiring supervisor may additionally additionally moreover you ask any question. I additionally tremendously suggest which you do a ridicule interview with an character which could offer comments in your solutions.

So now you have were given long long past thru the interview way and you start getting interest offers. That's amazing! But what do you do now? Do you are taking the number one project this is provided to you? Do you prevent interviewing altogether? Or do you retain? Those are all extraordinary questions and within the next segment I will screen the truth approximately approach offers that you need to understand in advance than you're taking delivery of a manner provide.

Revealing truths about mission gives.

Getting a way offer is thrilling! All the tough paintings that you mounted into locating a hobby has ultimately paid off. While that is brilliant there are certain topics that you have to keep in mind. First and primary, you want to understand that clearly because of the fact you get one system offer it doesn't propose you need to forestall interviewing. Even even though you do get a challenge offer you should hold interviewing for other positions. The motive being that you could likely come upon a better function with a tremendous pay. Also, with the useful useful resource of persevering with to interview, you can get extra hobby offers and then you can weigh your alternatives as to what business enterprise you need to paintings for.

The extraordinary component to keep in mind is that in spite of the reality that you do be given a hobby offer, it doesn't advocate which you have a mission. It genuinely method that you were extended a suggestion and also you took it however you need to although go through protocol and pass the clearance. The commercial agency agency can also additionally have a rigorous screening take a look at which also can embody a statistics take a look at, fingerprint test, or drug test and if you fail to skip any of those items, then don't get the approach. Therefore, it is in your super hobby to hold interviewing up until the on the spot which you are signing files and making all of it legitimate. I sincerely have labored with many clients that have been given a activity offer, stopped interviewing, and later they regretted their decision. This is precisely what passed off to a customer that I become supporting.

I labored with a extra youthful lady call Katie who had currently graduated with a maintain close's diploma and started out out challenge looking. She had three interviews scheduled in a single week and she or he or he come to be passionate about all 3 due to the reality they have been all incredible positions with amazing pay. Katie attended the primary interview and get on properly with the hiring manager. It went so properly for her that she have become employed right now. Katie modified into pleased with the position and the pay that she decided that she didn't want to interview for the opportunity positions. She called me and knowledgeable me of her selection. I tried explaining the advantages of going thru with the alternative interviews, but she wouldn't pay interest of it. She had made up her thoughts that she have come to be going with the primary undertaking. I knew that she turn out to be growing a mistake and that she might also sooner or later remorse it, however I furthermore knew that there wasn't anything I need to do approximately it.

Lo and behold, months later, I got a name from Katie to tell me that she wasn't glad at her new project. It have end up a toxic surroundings with internal strife, no communique, no experience of direction and she or he favored out. I knowledgeable her that there has been not a good buy that she need to do. Sure she might also want to move observe for emblem spanking new jobs however in the course of the interview approach they might ask her why she end up leaving a activity that she barely started. She didn't recognize a manner to answer to that question. There wasn't hundreds I may want to do for her, I suggest her to live with the organization for as a minimum one whole 365 days and then begin her challenge seek however she wasn't too glad with that response. This is the reason why I particularly recommend that a method seeker keep doing interviews up till the immediately that they start their new approach.

There you've got were given it, revealing truths which you want to understand approximately resumes, interest searching, interviewing, and system offers. Now you have got a better data of what you may be going up against at the identical time as seeking out your subsequent approach. I even have continuously said and maintain in thoughts that interest searching, while overwhelming and demanding, is not the toughest element. The hardest aspect is keeping your new method. I say this because of the truth at your new hobby you'll face many barriers that you may have to conquer so you will be successful. But don't fear because I have been given this problem recollect blanketed as properly.

Chapter 6: New Task

The first six months at your new task are important due to the reality that is the sink or swim part of your procedure. You are enthusiastic about your new process, and that's outstanding, however as speedy as that exuberant feeling fades away, reality will sink in and you may sense considered one of a type. I say this because while you're a part of a corporation, you will revel in the truth of it. You could be given assignments that you may have by no means finished. Or is probably requested to artwork on obligations that may be overwhelming In addition to this you need to moreover navigate a modern-day day surroundings in which you need to make your self familiar together with your colleagues and supervisors further to the employer's rules and pointers. And you ought to try this internal a focused time body.

The probation length can be as brief as ninety days or so long as three hundred and sixty five days. If you do not pass the probation length, you is probably given any other possibility in that you ought to expose yourself to the organization in any other case you is probably disregarded. In order to stay at the probation length at art work right here are a few hints that I especially recommend you examine;

Show up every single day, on time.

Do no longer call in ill, until it's miles a top emergency.

Do no longer refuse to do any form of project and responsibility. (even in case you are not positive the manner to do it.)

Do not get into any arguments collectively together with your coworkers.

Maintain a first rate and absolutely glad demeanor at all times.

Maintain a expert look constantly.

You is probably thinking to your self, properly those hints are not unusual sense and are clean to comply with and you're accurate they'll be. However in terms of a modern day way, you could see that many people, either don't recognize approximately those suggestions or do now not have a look at them and they become losing the project that they worked so hard to get. In addition to the above idea, I additionally pretty suggest maintaining your eyes and ears open and your mouth closed. Learn your surroundings, figure out who is who and what's what. Figure out who are the primary gamers and who're the assisting robust. The largest mistake that a extremely-present day employee can do is to go into a cutting-edge administrative center surroundings and act like they have got it all discovered. I can assure you that people do this may fall flat on their face.

Chapter 7: Understanding The Interview Process

In this starting bankruptcy, we embark on a adventure to very well understand the interview method, a critical element of every professional's career path. Interviews are frequently perceived as daunting hurdles, but they keep huge functionality for boom and possibility. This monetary catastrophe is designed to demystify the interview technique, providing clarity on what employers are seeking out and the way applicants can successfully exhibit their abilities and persona. By studying the underlying desires and dynamics of interviews, we're able to remodel them from intimidating encounters into attractive dialogues that open doorways to exciting career possibilities.

We start with the beneficial aid of exploring the middle purpose of interviews, presenting perception into the objectives and expectations of employers. This phase illuminates how interviews are not pretty much evaluating technical talents, but moreover approximately gauging cultural healthful, capacity for boom, and mutual compatibility. We then delve into the various styles of interviews, from traditional face-to-face meetings to the more and more famous video interviews, every requiring a nuanced technique. The bankruptcy concludes with an outline of the recruitment cycle, imparting a complete expertise of the adventure from software program submission to challenge provide. This foundational information is vital for everybody trying to navigate the interview panorama with self notion and poise.

The Purpose of Interviews

Understanding Employer Goals

At the heart of each interview lies the business enterprise organization's quest to discover the proper candidate. But what exactly are employers looking for?

Understanding those dreams is the first step in analyzing the interview method. Primarily, employers cause to test whether or not or now not or now not a candidate's capabilities and revel in align with the interest requirements. However, their evaluation extends beyond mere technical talents. Employers are also searching out applicants who display a sturdy work ethic, trouble-solving talents, and the functionality to adapt and grow inside the corporation. In essence, they attempting to find people who can make a contribution positively and correctly to the organisation's objectives and life-style.

Evaluating Fit: Skills, Culture, and Potential

The concept of 'healthful' in an interview context is multi-dimensional. First, there may be the alignment of talents and qualifications with the process's necessities. This is the maximum sincere detail of in shape, regularly assessed through a evaluate of your resume and particular procedure-related questions throughout the interview. But further crucial is cultural in shape – how properly your values, behaviors, and individual align with the enterprise agency's way of lifestyles. This is in which your studies into the corporation corporation's values and ethos pays off, allowing you to illustrate alignment with their way of life. Lastly, ability in shape is considered, which incorporates assessing your potential for increase, adaptability, and prolonged-term contribution to the corporation. Employers are eager on making an funding in people who display promise for destiny development and control.

Interviews as Two-Way Streets

Often disregarded, but essential to understand, is that interviews aren't pretty an awful lot being scrutinized; they're - manner interactions. As masses as it is an opportunity for the agency to assess you, it's miles further an opportunity a great way to determine the organization, the characteristic, and the humans you might be strolling with. Use this time to invite questions on the employer life-style, the group dynamics, the stressful conditions and opportunities of the location, and some different elements which might be essential to you in a activity. This technique now not exceptional demonstrates your proper interest and engagement but moreover enables you are making an knowledgeable choice must you get keep of a assignment offer. Remember, the intention of an interview isn't simply to get a hobby provide, but to find out a function and an business enterprise in which you could thrive and be happy.

Types of Interviews

Traditional, Behavioral, and Case Interviews

The panorama of interviews is severa, every type designed to evaluate particular factors of a candidate's suitability for a feature. Traditional interviews are the most commonplace and typically comprise a sequence of straightforward questions on your revel in, abilties, and qualifications. Behavioral interviews, on the other hand, delve into how you have got got had been given treated unique conditions within the past. These interviews perform on the premise that beyond conduct is the superb predictor of destiny standard normal performance. Questions regularly begin with "Tell me approximately a time while..." and require you to provide concrete examples. Case interviews are generally applied in consulting and organisation roles, in that you are provided with a commercial enterprise business enterprise problem and requested to advise a solution. This type tests your analytical talents, hassle-fixing approach, and the way you have a look at your statistics in realistic conditions.

Phone, Video, and In-Person Formats

The mode of an interview can appreciably have an effect on its dynamics. Phone interviews are frequently used as a initial screening tool. They require a focal point on clean verbal exchange and listening abilties, as you lack seen cues. Video interviews have end up increasingly familiar, specifically with the upward push of remote paintings. They combine factors of each mobile smartphone and in-character interviews, requiring you to be aware of each your verbal and non-verbal communique. Lastly, in-man or woman interviews provide a more holistic interplay, permitting each occasions to gauge compatibility extra effectively. Here, non-verbal cues, at the side of body language and eye contact, play a huge role.

Panel Interviews and Group Dynamics

Panel interviews include going through more than one interviewers right away. This layout is frequently used to assess how applicants have interaction with extremely good members of the organization or department and to accumulate severa views at the candidate's suitability. It's essential to engage with each panel member, every while responding and listening. Group interviews, however, involve more than one candidates being interviewed together. They are frequently used to evaluate teamwork, management, and interpersonal skills. In such settings, the challenge lies in fame out whilst additionally demonstrating your ability to art work collaboratively. It's a sensitive stability between showcasing your individual strengths and contributing definitely to the group.

The Recruitment Cycle

Timeline from Application to Offer

Understanding the recruitment cycle is vital for coping with expectations and preserving momentum to your device searching for. The journey begins with the software, in which your resume and cowl letter set the diploma. Following this, there can be a period of ready earlier than you pay interest once more, which could vary appreciably relying at the organization and the region. If your software program catches the business enterprise's hobby, the next section usually involves preliminary screening calls or interviews, which can be observed via secondary and every now and then tertiary rounds of interviews, often developing in specificity and intensity. After the final interview, there may be commonly a duration of evaluation through the hiring institution earlier than a suggestion is made. This entire manner can span weeks or perhaps months, highlighting the significance of staying power and staying electricity.

The Role of Human Resources and Hiring Managers

In the recruitment cycle, each human belongings (HR) professionals and hiring managers play pivotal roles. HR is generally chargeable for the preliminary tiers of the manner, which includes screening programs, coordinating interview schedules, and ensuring that the recruitment machine adheres to legal and organizational necessities. They are your number one problem of touch for logistical and procedural queries. The hiring supervisor, normally the possible supervisor or a senior employer member, turns into greater concerned in the later degrees. They consciousness on assessing the technical and cultural in form of applicants and make the very last hiring preference Understanding the ones roles will let you tailor your communique and questions appropriately at each degree.

Follow-up and Feedback Mechanisms

Navigating the submit-interview segment with professionalism can leave a protracted-lasting notable impact. Follow-up starts with a thank-you have a look at, preferably sent inside 24 hours of the interview. This gesture no longer satisfactory shows your appreciation but furthermore reaffirms your interest in the characteristic. If you haven't heard back in the time frame first of all communicated, it is suitable to ship a well mannered observe-up inquiry. Feedback mechanisms range among corporations. Some can also moreover provide certain comments for your interview primary overall performance, specially in case you've reached the final levels, even as others won't because of insurance constraints. Regardless, it is typically beneficial to courteously request comments, as it could offer precious insights for future interviews. Remember, every interplay in the recruitment cycle is an possibility to illustrate your professionalism and provide a lift on your suitability for the position.

Chapter 8: Preparing For The Interview

As we input the second one chapter, our focus shifts to one of the maximum essential components of the pastime-searching way: making geared up for the interview. This level is in which your basis starts offevolved offevolved, laying the muse for a a success interview revel in. Preparation is going some distance past rehearsing answers to common questions; it includes a entire technique encompassing research, self-mirrored image, and narrative development. In this financial ruin, we are able to manual you through each step, ensuring which you stroll into your interview ready not surely with solutions, however with an know-how of the employer, the function, and most significantly, your self. This holistic technique to steerage will now not extraordinary decorate your self warranty however furthermore notably increase your opportunities of creating a long lasting have an impact on.

Understanding the organisation employer and the feature you are the use of for is the cornerstone of effective schooling. This includes diving deep into the agency's lifestyle, values, and brand new tendencies, in addition to thoroughly analyzing the system description to recognize what the enterprise is simply on the lookout for. Equally critical is the approach of self-reflection—identifying your unique charge proposition, aligning your competencies and recollections with the goals of the placement, and crafting a compelling narrative that tells your tale in a way that resonates with the interviewer. By the give up of this bankruptcy, you will have a easy blueprint for making prepared for any interview, empowering you to offer yourself as a robust, nicely-rounded candidate who is not simply searching out any system, but the right pastime.

Researching the Company

Understanding the Company Culture and Values

To excel in an interview, it's far essential to understand the essence of the enterprise's manner of existence and values. This expertise no longer extremely good shapes your approach during the interview however furthermore lets in in figuring out if the organization aligns together collectively with your private and expert ethos. Start via way of exploring the commercial enterprise organization's website, paying near attention to sections like "About Us," "Mission Statement," and "Core Values Notice the language and topics that recur—do they emphasize innovation, teamwork, social responsibility, or patron popularity? Delve into their social media structures, blogs, and press releases for a extra dynamic and current-day view in their activities and public character. Additionally, systems together with Glassdoor and LinkedIn offer valuable insights via worker reviews and discussions, painting a image of the inner lifestyle and everyday art work surroundings.

Industry Trends and Company Position

A thorough information of the industry wherein the organisation operates and its position inside that organisation is in addition important. This expertise allows you to contextualize the business enterprise's techniques and annoying conditions, presenting a backdrop against which you can tailor your contributions. Begin through examining today's news, industry reviews, and exchange publications to understand cutting-edge-day trends, stressful situations, and innovations inside the place. Evaluate in which the enterprise stands on the subject of those developments: Are they a market chief, a challenger, a disruptor, or a gap participant? Awareness of the enterprise business enterprise's opposition and their marketplace strategies additionally can be insightful. This stage of enterprise statistics now not handiest demonstrates your entire guidance however additionally lets in you to have interaction in more sizable, knowledgeable discussions sooner or later of your interview.

Leveraging Information for Strategic Answers

Armed with a deep statistics of the agency's way of lifestyles, values, and employer role, you could now leverage this statistics to formulate strategic solutions. This method aligning your responses to reflect the business enterprise's values, showing how your non-public and professional characteristics make you a turning into addition to their organization. For example, if innovation is a middle fee of the business enterprise, spotlight your stories wherein you installed progressive questioning or led exchange initiatives. Similarly, facts of corporation developments will help you to speak how you could make contributions to addressing current-day-day traumatic situations or possibilities dealing with the enterprise corporation. The purpose is to provide yourself not really as a certified candidate, however as a person who actually is privy to and is enthusiastic about the opportunity of contributing to the commercial enterprise agency's vision and desires. This method transforms famous responses into compelling narratives that resonate together with your interviewers, placing you apart as a considerate and insightful candidate.

Understanding the Role

Job Description Analysis

The first step in getting ready for any interview is a meticulous assessment of the project description. This report is a goldmine of facts, outlining not most effective the obligations and expectancies of the location however moreover hinting on the underlying abilties and traits the agency is attempting to find. Start via breaking down the way description into key obligations and necessities. Look for repeated phrases or particular abilities which may be emphasized, as those are probably to be focal elements at some stage in the interview. It's furthermore important to study most of the strains—what does the method description suggest approximately the enterprise's priorities or the organization's way of life? Understanding those nuances will assist you tailor your responses to align with what the employer is simply looking for.

Required Skills and Competencies

Once you have dissected the approach description, emerge as privy to the specific talents and capabilities which can be vital for the role. These generally fall into education: difficult skills, which can be interest-particular competencies and records, and gentle talents, which includes verbal exchange, teamwork, and problem-solving. Assess how your private capacity set aligns with the ones necessities. Where you have direct revel in or abilties, plan the way to exhibit those effectively. For areas wherein your enjoy could now not proper now align, don't forget how your cutting-edge competencies should transfer or how your history has prepared you to fast studies and adapt. Demonstrating a proactive method to developing abilities you could presently lack also can be a effective way to show your dedication and boom mind-set.

Identifying Your Unique Value Proposition

Every candidate brings a completely unique aggregate of memories, capabilities, and views to the desk. Identifying your particular fee proposition includes facts what units you apart and the way this aligns with the desires of the function. Reflect on your personal and expert journey: What achievements are you most satisfied with? What demanding situations have you ever

ever overcome, and what have you ever ever determined out from them? How do your critiques provide you with a totally unique mind-set or method to the place you are making use of for? Articulate the ones elements in a way that connects your ancient beyond immediately to the fee you could deliver to the business enterprise. This isn't always quite tons assembly the baseline requirements of the method however approximately showcasing how your precise aggregate of talents, reports, and trends makes you an especially suitable suit for the position and the organisation.

Preparing Your Narrative

Crafting Your Story

A compelling narrative is a powerful tool in any interview. It consists of weaving together your reports, abilties, and aspirations right into a coherent and attractive tale that resonates collectively along with your interviewer. Start through figuring out the crucial component topics in your profession—moments of alternate, increase, or desire which have long-established your professional adventure. Consider how the ones opinions have organized you for the feature you are interviewing for. Your tale want to no longer be a recitation of your resume however instead a thoughtful choice of opinions that showcase your adventure, demanding situations, triumphs, and learnings. Aim for a narrative that is proper, reflective, and aligns with the feature and corporation lifestyle. This storytelling technique permits the interviewer see no longer genuinely what you have had been given finished, but who you are and the manner you approach paintings and existence.

Highlighting Achievements and Learning from Failures

Within your narrative, it is vital to strategically highlight key achievements. Choose examples that display off your capabilities and align with the task requirements. Quantify your successes everywhere feasible, as this gives credibility and permits the interviewer draw close to the impact of your art work. Equally essential is the functionality to speak approximately disasters or demanding conditions. The cause here isn't always to are living at the failure itself however to emphasize what you located from the experience and the manner it contributed for your expert increase. This indicates resilience, a functionality for self-mirrored image, and the capability to adapt and enlarge from setbacks—tendencies incredibly valued in any function.

Aligning Your Career Goals with the Company's Objectives

Finally, aligning your profession dreams with the organisation's dreams is a key element of making equipped your narrative. This includes not only expertise in which you need to move on your career however additionally how these aspirations healthy with the route and growth of the agency. For instance, if the business enterprise is known for innovation and you are searching for a function that allows for progressive trouble-fixing, spotlight this alignment. Or, if the agency is growing globally and you've got applicable worldwide experience or aspirations, make this connection smooth Demonstrating this alignment shows that you are not virtually looking for any venture, however which you are invested within the precise possibilities and worrying situations that include this role at this corporation. It's approximately growing a photo of mutual gain—a state of affairs in which your boom contributes to the agency's achievement, and vice versa.

Chapter 9: Crafting Effective Responses

Entering Chapter three, we flip our hobby to a critical talents within the interview device: crafting powerful responses. This monetary catastrophe is designed to equip you with the gadget and strategies vital to answer interview questions in a way this is each impactful and reflective of your actual capability. The assignment in an interview isn't truly to reply questions, but to do so in a manner that highlights your strengths, aligns with the agency's values, and differentiates you from unique candidates. We will guide you thru the nuances of various query kinds and percent techniques for structuring your responses in a manner that is attractive, relevant, and insightful.

In this chapter, we dissect the anatomy of various question patterns – from behavioral questions that probe into your past research to state of affairs-based absolutely questions that test your trouble-fixing abilties. Each kind of query requires a completely unique method, and studying the ones subtleties can drastically beautify the effectiveness of your responses. We will introduce frameworks much like the STAR technique for behavioral questions and discover strategies for articulating technical information with out getting out of place in jargon. Additionally, we delve into techniques for navigating greater tough factors of an interview, along side addressing sensitive subjects or responding to sudden questions. By the give up of this financial disaster, you will be higher organized to reveal every question into an possibility to exhibit your qualifications and in form for the position.

Behavioral Questions

STAR Method: Situation, Task, Action, Result

The STAR method is a mounted technique to answering behavioral interview questions, which are designed to evaluate your past conduct and reviews as symptoms of your destiny ordinary overall performance. The acronym STAR stands for Situation, Task, Action, and Result. To use this technique efficiently:

Situation: Begin by the usage of describing a selected scenario or context out of your past experience. Task: Next, provide an cause in the back of the undertaking or mission you have been confronted with in that situation. This clarifies your responsibility or the trouble you needed to treatment.

Action: Then, describe the actions you took to deal with the undertaking or project. Focus on what you probably did mainly, in region of what the group or institution did.

Result: Finally, percent the very last results of your actions. Highlight the excessive exceptional impact, what you discovered, or any reputation you received Quantifying effects, in which possible, can be particularly impactful.

Common Behavioral Questions and How to Approach Them

Behavioral questions often begin with phrases like "Tell me about a time even as..." or "Give me an instance of..." Some commonplace subjects include handling a difficult state of affairs or coworker, number one a challenge, or adapting to alternate. When coming near those questions, choose examples that no longer great display your capabilities applicable to the undertaking but also align with the enterprise organization's values and manner of lifestyles. Prepare recollections that show off pretty some abilities collectively with teamwork, management, initiative, and trouble-solving. Remember, the secret's to be precise and unique sufficient to offer a clean photograph of your characteristic and moves.

Demonstrating Emotional Intelligence and Problem-Solving Skills

Behavioral questions additionally provide an opportunity to exhibit your emotional intelligence and hassle-fixing abilties. When discussing interpersonal worrying conditions or institution dynamics, highlight the way you navigated those conditions with empathy, verbal exchange, and facts Similarly, whilst speakme about hassle-fixing conditions, attention to your analytical technique, the way you evaluated one-of-a-kind options, and your preference-making process. Demonstrating emotional intelligence entails displaying cognizance of your very own emotions and those of others, and the manner the ones have an effect on interactions and results. Through your examples, supply your capacity to control emotions correctly, collaborate with others, and adapt to converting situations.

Technical and Role-Specific Questions

Demonstrating Technical Competence

Technical and characteristic-particular questions are designed to assess your proficiency in the capabilities and information vital for the placement you're making use of for. When going thru those questions, it's essential to demonstrate your technical competence efficaciously. Prepare with the useful useful resource of reviewing the essential factor technical skills and know-how regions listed in the technique description. Consider modern-day initiatives or responsibilities in which you have executed these capabilities. When responding, use precise examples to illustrate your facts. For example, in case you're a software program software developer, describe a difficult coding task, the languages you used, and the very last effects of your paintings. The motive is to offer concrete proof of your technical abilities, showing the interviewer which you have the realistic skills needed to excel within the role.

Industry-Specific Knowledge and Skills

In addition to technical abilties, many roles require commercial enterprise enterprise-unique knowledge. This also can need to encompass familiarity with organization necessities, regulatory necessities, or marketplace dispositions. To prepare, studies the enterprise, that specialize in present day inclinations and the way they effect the function. If you've got direct industry enjoy, draw upon this, highlighting how your know-how and capabilities were accomplished in real-international conditions. If you are transitioning from each one of a kind industry, choose out transferable capabilities and memories, and articulate how those may be beneficial inside the new context. Demonstrating company-particular information shows the interviewer that you apprehend the wider context wherein the business enterprise operates and are prepared to contribute meaningfully from the start.

Balancing Detail with Clarity

One of the demanding situations in answering technical and role-unique questions is providing enough element to demonstrate your competence at the same time as although being clean and concise. Avoid overloading your answers with jargon or overly technical language, that might hard to apprehend your difficulty and lose the interviewer's hobby. Instead, goal to provide an reason of complex requirements or strategies in a manner that is available and comprehensible, even to a person who might not have a technical history. This capability is mainly crucial in roles that require pass-useful collaboration. It's about setting the proper stability: being distinct sufficient to reveal depth of information, yet clear and succinct sufficient to be results understood. This approach not only showcases your technical skills but additionally your potential to speak efficaciously, a key competency in any function.

Handling Tricky Questions

Addressing Salary Expectations

Questions about sales expectations may be a number of the most hard to navigate in an interview. It's essential to deal with these queries with a balance of honesty and strategic questioning. Before the interview, conduct studies to understand the everyday profits variety for the position in your enterprise and geographical area. This steerage permits you to offer an knowledgeable reaction. If driven for an early profits expectation, a tactful method is to precise your flexibility and interest within the position first, stating that you're open to discussing a reimbursement package deal that indicates the feature's responsibilities and your revel in. Alternatively, you could flip the query lower returned to the interviewer via way of asking about the budgeted revenue range for the location.

Navigating Past Work Experiences and Conflicts

Interview questions on previous art work research, specially the ones associated with conflicts or worrying situations, can be touchy. It's essential to technique these questions with a top notch and optimistic mindset. Focus on what you determined from the enjoy in choice to the warfare or trouble itself. Avoid speakme negatively about past employers or colleagues, as this could reflect poorly for your expert demeanor. Instead, frame the ones reviews as opportunities for growth and development, highlighting how they have prepared you for destiny roles. Your purpose is to illustrate your capacity to cope with place of work demanding situations with maturity and a solution-oriented mind-set.

Dealing with Hypothetical Scenarios

Hypothetical questions are utilized by interviewers to evaluate your trouble-solving skills, creativity, and functionality to assume for your toes. These questions would possibly probable encompass situations you haven't encountered earlier than, requiring you to apply your understanding and reasoning to indicate a ability answer. When responding to hypothetical situations, it is vital to stroll the interviewer through your idea system.

Chapter 10: Communication Skills And Body Language

In Chapter 4, we delve into the important factors of powerful communication and frame language inside the route of the interview way. Communication in interviews is going beyond truely the phrases you choose out; it encompasses the manner you are saying them, your body language, or maybe your listening abilties. This financial catastrophe is dedicated to helping you refine these elements to make sure your message is conveyed clearly, with a piece of luck, and convincingly. We discover various sides of verbal and non-verbal conversation, presenting insights and strategies to beautify your commonplace presentation. Whether you're interviewing in character, over the cellular telephone, or thru video, analyzing the ones abilities will considerably improve the affect you're making for your interviewers.

The first part of the chapter focuses on verbal verbal exchange. Here, we cowl the significance of clarity, conciseness, and self perception on your speech. We talk a manner to modulate your tone, pace, and amount to interact your interviewer and ensure your elements are understood. Additionally, we delve into the art work of powerful listening—a expertise frequently unnoticed but critical in demonstrating engagement and empathy in the direction of an interview. The second part of the monetary disaster addresses non-verbal communication. Body language, eye contact, or maybe your apparel play a huge function in how you are perceived. We provide guidance on dealing with fearful behavior, offering a expert demeanor, and using non-verbal cues to decorate your spoken phrases. By the prevent of this financial ruin, you'll be ready with the gadget to talk efficaciously in any interview setting, developing a superb and lasting affect.

Verbal Communication

Clarity, Conciseness, and Confidence

Effective verbal communication in an interview is characterised with the aid of clarity, conciseness, and self assurance. Clarity consists of expressing your thoughts in a straightforward and comprehensible manner, warding off jargon or overly complicated language that might confuse the interviewer. Conciseness is ready being succinct, respecting the interviewer's time with the resource of offering direct solutions without pointless information or tangents. This does now not propose oversimplifying your solutions, however rather focusing at the maximum relevant points. Confidence in communication is conveyed through a ordinary voice and confident language. It's now not just about what you are announcing however how you say it. Confidence can be evolved with workout; bear in mind rehearsing your solutions to commonplace interview questions and attempting to find comments from others to refine your shipping.

Tone of Voice and Articulation

The tone of your voice and your articulation appreciably effect how your message is obtained. Your tone need to be professional however approachable, adapting to the formality of the interview and the demeanor of the interviewer. Modulating your tone to emphasise key factors can also assist in making your message greater impactful. Articulation refers to how in reality you speak. Mumbling or speakme too swiftly could make it hard for the interviewer to conform with, on the same time as speaking too slowly may additionally propose a loss of self warranty or enthusiasm. Practice speakme at a measured pace and enunciating really to ensure your responses are without problem understood.

Effective Listening and Engagement

Listening is an often underestimated problem of powerful conversation in interviews. Demonstrating proper listening abilties suggests appreciate for the interviewer and guarantees you apprehend the questions being asked. It includes more than simply being attentive to the phrases; it's miles about actively attractive with the content. Show that you're listening thru using nodding, preserving eye touch, and responding efficiently to what's being said. Avoid interrupting and look ahead to a natural pause earlier than responding. Paraphrasing or summarizing the query earlier than answering also can show lively listening and make sure you are addressing the query correctly. Effective listening aids in building rapport with the interviewer and permits a greater interactive and engaging conversation.

Non-Verbal Communication

Body Language and Eye Contact

Non-verbal cues, in conjunction with frame language and eye touch, play a vital role in communique inside the path of an interview. Your frame language can bring self perception, openness, and attentiveness. Practice maintaining a extremely good posture, sitting upright however comfortable, and averting closed-off gestures like crossed fingers. Use hand gestures genuinely to emphasize points, however have in thoughts not to overdo them. Eye contact is similarly important; it demonstrates engagement and self assurance. In an in-person interview, maintain normal, but no longer non-forestall, eye contact collectively together with your interviewer. In a video interview, take a look at the digicam to simulate eye contact. However, it is also important to break eye contact from time to time to keep away from staring, which can be uncomfortable.

Dress Code and Professional Appearance

Your look is the first aspect an interviewer notices, and it units the tone for the interview. Dress as it ought to be for the enterprise and the place for that you are interviewing. If you are unsure of the company's dress code, err at the facet of professionalism. For guys, this might suggest a in shape or a button-down shirt with get dressed pants; for women, a in shape, dress, or professional shirt and skirt or pants. Ensure your clothes are clean, properly-turning into, and freed from wrinkles or excessive styles. Grooming is likewise a part of expert appearance, so be neat and tidy in your hairstyle, nails, and ordinary cleanliness. Remember, dressing professionally now not most effective makes a extraordinary first affect however also can enhance your self belief.

Managing Nervous Habits

It's herbal to revel in disturbing inside the route of an interview, but out of manage demanding conduct can be distracting.

These may in all likelihood include fidgeting, tapping your foot, gambling together with your hair, or excessively using filler phrases like "um" and "like." Becoming aware about your involved conduct is step one to managing them. Practice interviewing with a chum or in front of a mirror to come to be extra aware about those behaviors. Techniques like deep breathing or mindfulness can help calm nerves in advance than and at a few degree within the interview. If you discover your self starting to fidget, take a second to recenter your self, region your hands to your lap or at the table, and refocus on the communique. Managing the ones conduct will help you seem greater composed and confident at some stage in your interview.

Virtual Interview Etiquette

Technical Setup and Testing

In the generation of a long way flung artwork, digital interviews have come to be increasingly common. Ensuring a smooth technical setup is critical to avoid distractions and preserve professionalism. Prior to the interview, test your computer, webcam, microphone, and internet connection. Ensure your software, whether or not or not it is Zoom, Skype, or each other platform, is updated and functioning efficaciously. Conduct a trial run with a friend or family member to test that your audio and video are clean. Also, ensure your device is plugged in or really charged to avoid power interruptions. Having a backup plan, at the side of a secondary tool organized, also may be beneficial in case of surprising technical problems.

Background and Environment

The bodily surroundings seen sooner or later of your digital interview can effect the interviewer's affect. Choose a quiet, nicely-lit location wherein you could not be interrupted. Your historical past need to be neat and expert; a definite wall or a tidy, uncluttered area works well. Be privy to the lighting fixtures—natural slight is right, but if that is now not viable, ensure the lights within the room does no longer solid harsh shadows or glare. Additionally, adjust your virtual digital camera attitude to be at eye diploma, which allows in maintaining a greater herbal and tasty eye touch during the communication.

Virtual Presence and Engagement Strategies

Maintaining presence and engagement in a digital interview requires aware try. Position the camera just so your pinnacle body is seen, permitting you to apply hand gestures glaringly. Since you are now not inside the same room, it is vital to be even extra expressive along side your facial expressions and tone of voice to deliver enthusiasm and engagement. Nod and smile to show you're actively listening. When speaking, be smooth and barely slower than ordinary to account for functionality audio delays. Minimize distractions via closing needless computer packages and silencing your cellphone. Demonstrating your comfort with digital verbal exchange now not handiest displays your adaptability but moreover your professionalism in contemporary virtual art work surroundings.

Chapter 11: The Day Of The Interview

As we embark on Chapter 5, we focus on a pivotal 2nd for your process seek journey: the day of the interview. This financial disaster is dedicated to guiding you through the final preparations and techniques to make certain you are at your superb on this crucial day. It's a time at the same time as all of your research, education, and practice converge to offer you because the high-quality candidate for the placement. We will discover the way to superb-music your training, manage logistical additives, and mentally put together yourself to go into the interview with self notion and composure. This financial ruin isn't pretty a whole lot what to do on the day of the interview, however additionally about how to be—a way to embody the developments and thoughts-set a good way to make you stand out as a candidate.

The first part of this financial disaster addresses the realistic troubles for the day of your interview. We'll speak the importance of reviewing key factors out of your research and preparations, and the manner to make certain all logistical facts—like timing, commands, and attire—are meticulously deliberate. These factors, while apparently minor, can substantially effect your united states of thoughts and overall performance in the path of the interview. The 2nd part delves into intellectual and emotional guidance. We discover strategies for dealing with strain and nerves, a way to domesticate a nice attitude, and strategies for staying conscious and present all through the interview. By the cease of this financial ruin, you'll be organized not definitely with a checklist of things to do, but with a framework for the manner to approach the interview day with a balanced, assured, and targeted thoughts-set.

Final Preparations

Reviewing Key Points and Research

On the eve of your interview, it's miles crucial to check the critical component factors and research you've got got had been given compiled. Go via your notes approximately the employer, the approach description, and any relevant employer dispositions. Refresh your memory on the examples and stories you have got were given organized to illustrate your skills and stories, that specialize in folks who align most cautiously with the project requirements and business employer manner of lifestyles. This examine should not be approximately cramming; it's extra approximately reaffirming your facts and getting your key factors sparkling on your thoughts. A calm, centered evaluation can boom your self assurance and ensure that you're geared up to weave this records clearly into your responses at a few level within the interview.

Practical Considerations: Timing, Directions, and Attire

Attention to sensible records can appreciably lessen pressure at the day of the interview. Plan your outfit in advance, selecting attire that is professional and suitable for the economic employer organization tradition. Ensure the whole lot is simple, pressed, and laid out geared up to position on. If the interview is in-person, double-check the interview place, plan your direction, and decide how lengthy the adventure will take. It's surely beneficial to permit more time for surprising delays. If the interview is virtual, verify your era setup once more and make sure your place is quiet and interruption-loose. In each conditions, purpose to be prepared as a minimum 15 minutes in advance than the scheduled time to permit yourself a 2d to loosen up and collect your thoughts.

Mindfulness and Stress-Reduction Techniques

It's ordinary to revel in worried in advance than an interview, however dealing with the ones nerves is vital for highest first-class regular average performance. Techniques at the side of deep respiration, meditation, or slight bodily exercise can be powerful in lowering pressure. Practice mindfulness carrying sports activities to middle your self and domesticate a experience of calm. Visualizing a a achievement interview also may be a effective device to beautify yourself notion. On the morning of the interview, engage in a ordinary that makes you experience snug and first-rate – whether or not or not that's a quick stroll, taking note of music, or a cup of your selected tea or espresso. Remember, a non violent and composed mind will can help you suppose clearly and gift your remarkable self at a few diploma within the interview.

During the Interview

Making a Strong First Impression

The preliminary moments of your interview could have an extended-lasting effect on how the interviewer perceives you. A sturdy first effect is crafted from several elements: a assured greeting, a company handshake (in in-man or woman interviews), and a warmth, real smile. Dress appropriately for the employer lifestyle, as your look plays a aspect on this initial evaluation. In a virtual interview, make certain you are positioned within the the front of the virtual digicam a couple of minutes in advance than the scheduled time, ready to greet the interviewer right away. Pay interest on your body language inside the course of; preserve specific posture, steady eye touch, and use gestures truely to particular yourself. The secret's to carry self notion, professionalism, and exuberance for the position from the outset.

Navigating the Conversation

Once the interview is underway, awareness on navigating the communication effectively. This includes actively paying attention to the questions, taking a second to compose your mind in advance than responding, and answering in a way this is each concise and informative. Remember the crucial element factors you prepared and search for opportunities to weave them into your responses virtually. Be honest on your solutions; in case you do not recognize a few aspect, it's far higher to admit it and show a willingness to investigate. Adapt your verbal exchange style to the go along with the float of the communication – if the interviewer is formal, in shape their tone; if they will be extra conversational, experience unfastened to reciprocate even as very last professional.

Asking Insightful Questions

An interview is a -manner street, and asking insightful questions is an important part of the technique. It demonstrates your interest inside the position and the organization, and it gives you vital records that will help you decide if the project and culture are a brilliant healthy for you. Prepare a listing of questions in advance, but moreover be geared up to invite spontaneous ones primarily based at the interview verbal exchange. Inquire about particular components of the activity, the institution you may be running with, the employer's destiny plans, or the manner of life. Avoid asking questions whose answers are resultseasily decided on the agency's net site or favored queries that don't show deep engagement with the characteristic or enterprise. Well-idea-out questions can leave a strong have an impact on and make your interview memorable.

Post-Interview Protocol

Thank-You Notes and Follow-Ups

After the interview, it's far vital to send a thank-you study to the interviewer(s). This need to be finished internal 24 hours of the interview. A well-crafted thank-you be aware reiterates your interest in the role, indicates on a key a part of the interview communication, and reinforces why you're a sturdy candidate for the location. It's now not handiest a gesture of courtesy however moreover an possibility to make one very last, great have an effect on. If you have not heard returned within the time-body first of all mentioned, it is suitable to deliver a polite observe-up e-mail. This e-mail must specific your persisted interest inside the position and inquire approximately the popularity of the hiring machine. Remember to keep your observe-usaexpert and concise.

Reflecting on Performance and Feedback

Post-interview mirrored image is a precious workout, irrespective of the final effects. Take some time to evaluate your standard overall performance. What went well? What could have been progressed? Think about the questions you responded strongly and those that stuck you off defend. This mirrored image will help you perceive areas for improvement and prepare you for destiny interviews. If you are not a fulfillment, do now not hesitate to ask the interviewer or HR representative for feedback. While no longer all organizations provide particular feedback, any insights offered may be rather beneficial for your professional growth and destiny interview steering.

Handling Offers and Negotiations

If you get maintain of a mission offer, make the effort to review it very well. Consider all aspects of the provide, which consist of earnings, advantages, artwork hours, organization culture, and the precise responsibilities of the area. If there are regions you are not glad with, or if the offer differs from your expectancies, you could want to enter into negotiations. Be smooth and low-priced for your requests.

Chapter 12: Navigating Special Situations

In Chapter 6, we flip our interest to navigating specific situations in interviews – conditions that won't be famous but are an increasing number of common in nowadays's various and dynamic job marketplace. This financial destroy is dedicated to equipping you with the abilities and insights crucial to address particular interview times with a chunk of success and correctly. Whether you're returning to the employees after a vast hollow, moving industries, or coping with an interview in an sudden cultural context, this financial disaster gives tailored strategies to cope with those worrying situations. Understanding a way to offer your research and abilties in the ones conditions can make a sizable difference in how you are perceived via capability employers.

We begin by means of the use of way of exploring the manner to correctly speak profession gaps or transitions. This includes strategies for framing intervals of unemployment or career breaks surely, emphasizing the talents and stories obtained at some stage in those times. We then delve into the nuances of interviewing for positions in industries precise out of your beyond revel in, specializing in a way to recognition on transferable competencies and versatility. The chapter additionally covers the intricacies of global and far flung venture interviews, imparting guidance on cultural troubles, etiquette, and demonstrating worldwide competency. By the cease of this monetary ruin, you can have a complete knowledge of a way to technique those precise interview conditions, enabling you to encompass and leverage your precise career direction as a electricity.

Career Gaps and Transitions

Addressing Periods of Unemployment

Career gaps, whether or not because of non-public reasons, layoffs, or profession breaks, are a not unusual a part of many professional journeys. When addressing durations of unemployment in an interview, honesty and positivity are key. Be sincere about the purpose for the space, specializing in what you placed or carried out at some point of this time. For instance, in case you took time without work for personal improvement or to pursue education, highlight how this has organized you higher for the employees. If the distance modified into due to instances beyond your control, which includes a layoff, emphasize your resilience and proactive steps taken closer to re-stepping into the workforce, like upskilling or volunteering. The goal is to border those intervals no longer as setbacks, but as precious reviews which have contributed in your private and expert increase.

Career Pivots and Changing Industries

Transitioning to a cutting-edge enterprise can be hard, however it additionally demonstrates flexibility and a willingness to analyze. When discussing a career pivot in an interview, consciousness at the reason in the back of the exchange. Articulate your passion for the brand new enterprise and the way your preceding reviews have led you to this selection. It's crucial to attract parallels amongst your beyond roles and the handiest you are interviewing for, showing how your competencies and opinions are relevant and transferable. Explain how your precise heritage can supply a sparkling attitude to the position. Employers fee severa reports, so highlight how your severa career path is an asset.

Highlighting Transferable Skills

One of the handiest strategies at the identical time as transitioning careers or re-getting into the frame of personnel is to emphasize your transferable talents. These are capabilities which can be precious during various industries and roles, together with control, communication, hassle-fixing, and project manage. Identify the middle abilties required in the new feature and draw connections on your preceding studies, demonstrating how the ones capabilities were honed over your profession. Provide precise examples of methods you've got applied those skills in special contexts, and the way they can be beneficial in the new role. By specializing in those adaptable skills, you may feature your self as a bendy and valuable candidate, even in case your direct enjoy in the agency is restrained.

International and Remote Interviews

Cultural Considerations and Etiquette

In nowadays's global interest market, worldwide interviews are more and more not unusual, and that they often require an hobby of cultural nuances and etiquette. When making organized for an international interview, studies the cultural norms and business company practices of the u . S . In which the employer is based totally definitely. This can include knowledge communique styles (direct rather than oblique), attitudes towards punctuality, and appropriate sorts of deal with. Be privy to variations in frame language and gestures, as these can range appreciably throughout cultures. In the interview, display your admire for those cultural norms. For instance, in some cultures, it's preferred to interact in small talk before taking off to business enterprise, at the same time as in others, such directness is favored. Showing your cultural consciousness not handiest allows in constructing rapport but additionally demonstrates your ability to conform and paintings efficiently in a global surroundings.

Demonstrating Global Competency

Global competency consists of statistics and respecting unique cultural perspectives, being adaptable, and owning the ability to paintings correctly with human beings from severa backgrounds. In an international interview, exhibit your worldwide competency by discussing any worldwide studies you have got, along with studying or working remote places, getting to know a 2d language, or strolling with global agencies. Highlight your capacity to navigate cross-cultural communication and the manner you've efficiently managed or tailored to cultural variations. These opinions and abilties are pretty valued in nowadays's interconnected global and can set you apart as a candidate who can make contributions to a diverse and international body of employees.

Discussing Remote Work Dynamics

With the upward push of a long way flung work, many interviews moreover consciousness to your capability to work independently and correctly in a far off setting. Be prepared to talk about your enjoy with a long way flung artwork, if applicable. Talk approximately the manner you organize your day, speak with group individuals, and live efficient and encouraged outdoor of a traditional place of job environment. If you haven't had a good buy a long way flung paintings enjoy, recognition on related abilties which includes time management, self-motivation, and talent with digital collaboration device. You also can talk techniques you may placed into impact to conquer not unusual a long way off work demanding situations, inclusive of isolation or maintaining artwork-lifestyles balance. Demonstrating which you are adaptable and effective in a far flung artwork placing is more and more important within the modern assignment panorama.

Unique Industry Requirements

Creative Fields and Portfolio Reviews

In modern fields like image design, architecture, or content material material material creation, a portfolio evaluation is usually a applicable a part of the interview gadget. Your portfolio want to be a carefully curated series of your artwork that showcases your skills, creativity, and style of reviews. Before the interview, tailor your portfolio to the hobby you are utilising for, highlighting obligations that align with the commercial enterprise corporation's fashion or the ideal position. Be organized to speak approximately every piece for your portfolio in element, together with your progressive manner, the demanding conditions you faced, and the way you overcame them. This communicate offers perception into your trouble-fixing competencies and progressive wondering. It's moreover an possibility to demonstrate your passion for your work and your capability to articulate your ideas absolutely.

Technical Professions and Coding Tests

For technical professions, especially in software program software improvement or engineering, coding tests or technical demanding situations are a common part of the interview approach. These assessments determine your technical talents, hassle-solving capability, and every now and then, your capacity to work below time constraints. To prepare, exercise with coding annoying conditions or duties much like the ones you may stumble upon inside the interview. Familiarize yourself with the agency's technology stack and the particular competencies said within the interest description. During the test, take note of writing easy, inexperienced code and report your belief approach. If you come upon problems, articulate how you're looking for to treatment the trouble, as this may be simply as informative for the interviewer as a correct solution.

Consulting Case Interviews

In consulting, case interviews are a completely particular and difficult difficulty of the hobby interview technique. These interviews take a look at your analytical wondering, commercial employer acumen, and hassle-solving approach. You'll be provided with a agency trouble and asked to speak about how you'll resolve it. To prepare, exercise with some of case studies and familiarize yourself with commonplace enterprise company frameworks. During the interview, take a 2d to shape your mind earlier than diving into the hassle. Ask clarifying questions if wanted, and walk the interviewer thru your notion system as you dissect the case. Focus on demonstrating a logical, mounted approach to problem-fixing. Remember, communication is fundamental – present your thoughts simply and concisely, and be prepared to speak approximately and protect your conclusions.

Chapter 13: Advanced Interview Techniques

In Chapter 7, we beautify our attention to superior interview techniques, diving into strategies that might set you apart as a standout candidate in a aggressive method marketplace. This financial spoil is designed for humans who've mastered the basics of interviewing and are simply trying to refine their approach, add intensity to their responses, and make a memorable impact on their interviewers. Here, we find out the nuances of strategic storytelling, contemporary negotiation techniques, and the paintings of constructing lasting expert relationships. These superior talents are important for certainly all people trying to no longer just steady a method, however to excel of their profession and set up themselves as a treasured asset in any professional setting.

We start thru delving into the power of strategic storytelling—a method that transforms your testimonies and qualifications into compelling narratives. This phase wills manual you at the way to weave your competencies, achievements, and profession aspirations into stories that resonate deeply alongside facet your interviewers, developing an emotional connection and a long lasting affect. Following this, we tackle the regularly-daunting element of sales negotiation, equipping you with techniques to with a bit of accurate fortune negotiate your really well worth even as keeping a extraordinary relationship with capacity employers. Lastly, we hobby on the importance of constructing and maintaining professional relationships through the interview way Whether it's networking with interviewers or leveraging the interview experience for destiny possibilities, this bankruptcy gives profitable insights into developing a community that permits and enhances your lengthy-time period career trajectory.

Strategic Storytelling

Using Stories to Illustrate Competencies

Strategic storytelling is a effective tool in interviews, allowing you to carry your abilties and reviews to life in a manner that is each attractive and terrific. The secret's to select tales that successfully illustrate the abilities and attributes most applicable to the area you're making use of for. These memories ought to offer concrete examples of the way you have finished your talents in actual-global situations, demonstrating your hassle-fixing capabilities, management tendencies, teamwork, or adaptability. When crafting these memories, popularity on particular challenges you confronted, the actions you took, and the consequences of these actions, ensuring they align with the capabilities the business enterprise is searching out. Well-determined on testimonies make your talents greater tangible and relatable, allowing the interviewer to study you within the position.

Balancing Professionalism with Personality

While professionalism is paramount in an interview placing, infusing your responses with a touch of your person may additionally want to make you extra relatable and go away an extended-lasting have an effect on. Your memories ought to no longer only mirror your professional achievements but furthermore provide insights into your individual, values, and the characteristics that make you specific. This balance can be executed by sharing reviews that display screen your passion, your motivations, or moments in which your non-public tendencies finished a key position to your expert success. However, it is critical to hold a expert tone and ensure that the anecdotes are applicable to the technique and company lifestyle. The intention is to provide yourself as a nicely-rounded candidate who not handiest has the essential competencies and enjoy however furthermore brings a totally precise and precious angle to the team.

Engaging and Persuasive Communication

The effectiveness of strategic storytelling additionally hinges on your capacity to speak in a captivating and persuasive way. This involves being easy, concise, and articulate, ensuring your stories are easy to have a look at and compelling. Use vibrant descriptions and feelings to deliver your memories to existence, but avoid pointless statistics that would detract from the primary message. Your transport need to be assured and enthusiastic, displaying which you're truly obsessed with your studies and the opportunity of bringing similar charge to the present day day position. Additionally, the usage of persuasive language that aligns with the organisation's dreams and values can assist the interviewer see the direct benefits of your contributions. By mastering attractive and persuasive storytelling, you could redesign a favored interview into a memorable communique that underscores your suitability for the placement.

Negotiating Offers

Understanding Your Worth

A important problem of any method provide negotiation is understanding and articulating your actually really worth. Before stepping into negotiations, conduct thorough research to recognize the enterprise-popular income for the location, considering elements like your experience, geographic place, and the dimensions of the industrial employer business enterprise. Reflect on your unique abilities, reports, and the cost you deliver to the feature. Recognizing your really worth now not high-quality facilitates in setting realistic expectations but additionally boosts yourself guarantee within the negotiation way. Prepare to articulate your qualifications and the way they align with the corporation's desires, the usage of particular examples from your career to enhance your elements. This knowledge forms the concept of a robust, justified argument for the compensation you're attempting to find.

Discussing Benefits and Flexibility

Negotiating a interest provide isn't always quite a superb deal earnings; it moreover includes discussing benefits and specific styles of reimbursement. These can encompass clinical medical insurance, retirement plans, paid time off, far off paintings options, expert development opportunities, and additional. Determine which blessings are most vital to you and be organized to speak about those at a few stage inside the negotiation way. In some instances, companies may be greater flexible with benefits than with earnings. Additionally, keep in mind negotiating for flexibility in art work preparations, especially if far flung or hybrid art work is crucial to you. Understanding the complete scope of the repayment bundle lets in for a more holistic negotiation method, wherein you may balance particular factors ordinary together together with your private and professional priorities.

Strategies for Salary Negotiation

When it entails income negotiation, technique the conversation with a stability of assertiveness and international members of the family. Initiate the discussion with the beneficial useful resource of expressing your enthusiasm for the place and the enterprise. When presenting your income expectancies, provide a choice instead of a specific variety, based on your research and records of your in reality truly worth. This gives room for dialogue and indicates your willingness to barter. Be organized to reply to counteroffers and justify your request with clean purpose. It's essential to pay attention actively to the organisation's attitude and live open to compromise. Remember, negotiation is a -way communication aimed towards accomplishing a at the same time great agreement. Throughout the technique, keep a expert demeanor, and avoid ultimatums or confrontational language, as the motive is to installation a first rate foundation for your future operating relationship.

Long-Term Relationship Building

Networking with Interviewers

Building relationships together together with your interviewers may be a strategic waft, irrespective of the instantaneous final results of the interview. See every interaction as an opportunity to extend your professional community. Approach the interview as a communication wherein you and the interviewer have a examine each precise. Even in case you do no longer get the activity, leaving a extraordinary effect can result in future opportunities. After the interview, hold in mind connecting with the interviewers on professional networks like

LinkedIn, expressing your gratitude for the possibility and your hobby in retaining in touch. This can help you live on their radar for future positions or commercial enterprise enterprise insights. Remember, networking is ready mutual advantage, so be open to presenting fee in go back, retaining the relationship balanced and professional.

Leveraging Interviews for Future Opportunities

Every interview experience, irrespective of its final consequences, is a studying possibility and a stepping stone for destiny fulfillment. Reflect to your regular common performance and discover areas for development. If you aren't decided on for the feature, don't hesitate to invite the interviewer for remarks that will help you in future packages. Additionally, maintain a tremendous dating with the business enterprise. Express your persevered hobby within the corporation and ask to be taken into consideration for destiny roles that align together with your abilities and experience. Staying in contact with the corporation via periodic updates for your professional achievements can keep you on their radar for at the equal time because the right possibility arises.

Building a Professional Reputation

Your conduct inside the direction of the interview method contributes drastically for your professional popularity. Always approach interactions with professionalism, recognize, and integrity. This includes being responsive for your communications, punctual and prepared for interviews, and courteous for your follow-ups. Additionally, actively contribute on your area via systems like enterprise forums, blogs, or social media. Sharing your insights, taking element in discussions, and networking with friends can assist set up you as a informed and engaged expert. A strong reputation for your commercial enterprise business enterprise can result in recruiters on the lookout for you out for possibilities and might open doors to roles that might not be publicly marketed.

Chapter 14: Preparing For The Interview

Find out as much as you could about the assignment, the agency, and the interview.

The particulars of the pastime, the business employer, or maybe who is sporting out the interview and the way will play a tremendous function for your interview training.

1. Examine the organization.

Put in a couple of hours gaining all that you can approximately the enterprise — from but many property as you can. Read the most current press releases, communicate to people in your network about finding contemporary-day and previous employees, and high quality, and spend a while on Google. Most of the time, applicants simplest check what a agency posts on its net net web page and social media payments, not at what different people are pronouncing. You can be prepared to speak approximately why you would really like to artwork there and what you can do for them if you check more than one resource. You might also moreover get a greater entire image of the corporation, inclusive of any terrible press.

2. Find out as a top notch deal as you could about the to be had function.

You need to recognize what the interviewer is seeking out earlier than you can showcase to them why you may be a wonderful rent. Fortunately, most establishments have spread out precisely actual factor they need in a candidate within the gig posting. Therefore, pass lower back to the outline that you examined prior to the usage of. What reminiscences and competencies are they that specialize in? What troubles must this new rent remedy? Throughout your interview, you must emphasize those factors.

three. Evaluate the agency's object or management (if possible).

Try the product (ideally some instances) earlier than your interview if the business enterprise you're interviewing for gives it. Being someone yourself is step one in accomplishing your goal of making fee for those who use that product if you are employed. In addition, it'll assist with showing the the usage of administrator that you're in reality eager on the interest.

4. Without appearing creepy, discover approximately the interviewers.

Ask who you may be assembly with in some unspecified time in the future of your interview if you aren't advised. Learn about every interviewer's role at the organization and prepare some questions for them. You can inquire approximately specifics of their assignment, talk approximately recent happenings of their location, or deliver up a common interest they've outside of the administrative center (honestly make certain it's far mentioned in a place that is easy to discover, like their LinkedIn profile or employer bio).

five. Prepare consequently based totally on the sort of interview you may be participating in.

Ask approximately the styles of interviews which is probably utilized by first-rate corporations. For instance, a few companies will will let you meet one-on-one with more than one personnel, on the equal time as others also can require you to give an interview presentation or meet with a couple of humans simultaneously. Additionally, you may have a video or phone interview. It is absolutely right to inquire in advance approximately the interview format from the HR contact or recruiter. And whilst you are aware about it, taking the time to find out approximately this style should make a big distinction.

Learn extra about interview questions and techniques.

Utilizing what you have got decided out, you have to then exercise answering commonplace interview questions and the use of interview techniques.

6. Determine the advantages you bring to the position.

Regardless of whether or no longer you're a completely heaps oiled assembly tool, it's essential to make investments strength considering carefully about what competencies, achievements, and interview solutions will resound with your questioners maximum for this artwork. What are your management abilities? Your originality? Examine the additives of your studies that high-quality qualify you.

7. Prepare to provide an reason for yourself to the interviewer.

You have to prepare a tailored and prepared-to-pass response to the query "Tell me about yourself" for every and each interview. You need to make sure you're getting off to a superb begin because interviewers almost usually ask questions like "Walk me through your resume" to start the communication.

8. Find out why you're interested by this organisation's feature.

You will in all likelihood be asked why you are interested in this function and organization. And you shouldn't be inside the interview if you may't answer this query!!) Therefore, to make sure that you may be able to respond, endure in mind a few key factors of the task and the commercial enterprise employer which can be in accurate alignment together at the side of your strengths, pastimes, and/or paintings fashion and make you captivated with the vicinity. You can use this to inform your responses to exceptional questions even in case you aren't mainly requested approximately this.

9. Do a few research on salaries.

You is probably requested about your earnings expectations even if you aren't organized to speak approximately cash. Do some profits research to decide out how you will reply to keep away from being stuck off guard and giving (or agreeing to) a number of that is manner too low.

10. Get your memories organized.

The majority of interviewers will ask you at the least some behavioral questions, which is probably approximately how you've got got behaved inside the beyond or how you may behave in sure situations. You can put together a few memories approximately your previous paintings reports that you could adapt as wanted, but you can't expect each possible situation.

11. Learn the STAR technique for your self.

When you inform a story to reply interview questions, you need to make certain the takeaway is apparent and the tale is well based. Your goal must be to answer the query truly and concisely on the same time as concurrently supplying your interviewer with all the context they require to realize what happened. Using the STAR approach is one method. STAR denotes:

Situation: Momentarily spread out the situation utilizing slightly enough element that the questioner will understand the stakes and all of the other subjects to your response.

Task: Discuss your function in the circumstance.

Action: Describe what you did and why.

Result: Describe the final results and what you determined out on your interviewer.

Keep in thoughts that you can need to slightly modify this shape for some questions. Consider first defining what leadership method to you earlier than discussing a time when you verified management skills, as an instance.

However, the STAR approach will assure that your memories will constantly have a starting, middle, and give up.

12. Make a list of important statistics and numbers.

Pay hobby to the numbers! You can use any sort of metrics, which includes engagement rates, budget or group sizes, chances of time saved, or something else, to illustrate your effect. When answering behavioral interview questions or talking about your responsibilities and accomplishments, inclusive of a few tough numbers honestly sweetens the deal and facilitates you provide an purpose for to a hiring manager why you are so exquisite. You want to record them on paper so you can allude to them in some unspecified time in the future of the assembly. (Even in case you don't paintings with numbers, proper right here's a manner to quantify your achievements.)

Thirteen. Improve your interviewing competencies.

Although it's far big, how properly you respond to interview questions isn't the whole lot. Other interview abilities like lively listening, small talk, and empathy also are being picked up on by the usage of manner of interviewers, both consciously or unconsciously. These skills no longer simplest assist you impress the interviewer, however moreover they display them what it might be want to artwork with you.

14. Your responses to not unusual interview questions must be practiced, but no longer memorized.

You should and may exercising answering common interview questions, but you shouldn't write down your entire reaction. Instead, make some short notes or bullet elements and produce them with you to the interview. Without reading from a script, you'll ensure you cover all the bases.

Practice answering them aloud at the equal time as searching within the replicate. This art work will help you decided in reality and make you feel a good deal extra relaxed at a few level in the interview.

15. Ponder non-verbal conversation.

Learn greater approximately how exceptional frame language is conveyed. Check your stance and posture to peer if they're conveying the right message. Sitting collectively with your legs and arms crossed, as an example, conveys a sense of defensiveness or isolation.) Consider your moves beforehand of time to avoid being distracted inside the direction of the interview. Think about the manner you'll display that you're actively taking part in that format in case you're on video. For instance, you may place the Zoom window near your digital digital camera so that you don't appearance a ways from your interviewer, or you can make nonverbal gestures or expressions to show which you're listening without lowering off their microphone.

16. Try some exercise interviews.

Do some mock interviews with a chum or cherished one when you have the time. When requested, "What may you convey to the position?" you'll be masses better organized. Whilst you do it a hundred instances, you can already understand in which you need to sit and positioned your fingers.

17. Record questions you'll ask them.

The everyday query on the prevent of an interview is, "Do you've got were given any questions for me?" likewise, you want to simply have some inquiries. You can begin through asking the questions about this list of interview questions, however you have to moreover plan a few questions which can be very unique to the place and the employer. You should also prepare more than you found you may need because of the reality you don't need to invite questions which have already been replied or run out of alternatives if the interviewer has already responded your first questions.

18. Make a plan for what you'll do in case you are amazed.

You can't get equipped for the whole lot, except you could plan to deal with the unexpected — like an inquiry question you don't have any concept a way to reply. If you need time to stall and accumulate your mind, for example, you can give you a pass-to word to help you keep away from vain talk. Repeating the query thoughtfully earlier than responding or affirming, slowly, "Now, that may be a incredible question" are effective techniques. I count on I might have to mention..." Prepare for expertise or technical interview questions.

Start making prepared and walking towards as rapid as you can if you're going to a technical interview or if you've been knowledgeable there can be a skill test. You will not exceptional get suitable exercise via the use of jogging through a prep e book or pattern questions, however you may furthermore get into the proper mind-set for fixing problems.

Get organized to do a super technique of imparting yourself and decide out all the data of the interview.

After you've got organized for the content fabric of your interview, it's time to make certain which you arrive on the interview searching polished and assured.

20. Decide what to put on.

You want to don't forget your physical look except you are getting prepared for a cellular phone interview. Yes, pants are required for video interviews.) Have no concept what to vicinity on? If you don't have already got one, discover a touch at the agency or have a look at pics on their Instagram or Muse profile, and get dressed at least as professionally as employees do. Business informal, as an instance, is appropriate for an interview in a informal setting.

21. Appear professional and appropriate.

Keep the little matters in thoughts. Clean, iron, or steam your outfit, and if essential, have it tailor-made (a present day match is fantastic). Sparkle your shoes, take a look at without cost sews, and make sure your fingernails appearance slick. Do instead spoiling, since putting your extraordinary self beforehand assists you with feeling your exceptional. Go for it if this means that you want a facial, haircut, shave, or possibly a modern-day outfit in your interview! If you could't manage to pay for the proper outfit, you can visit a Goodwill or thrift preserve nearby or look for offerings on your location that supply out-of-paintings humans free or discounted interview clothing. Your self belief will boom in case you experience suitable about yourself, and also you possibly already recognize that self assurance is vital to getting the interest.

22. Make duplicates of your resume.

If you'll an in-character interview, you need to carry sufficient copies of your resume for every of the humans you are meeting with and one replica for yourself to consult. However, printing a tough reproduction of your resume so you can without difficulty check with it sooner or later of a cellular phone or video interview can although be beneficial.

23. Make a list of references.

Set up a reference listing, regardless of whether or not or now not you suspect you'll be requested it. Include the name, call, organization, branch or department, smartphone range, and email deal with of every reference, similarly to a sentence describing the connection in brief (as an example, "Carlton modified into my organization leader for 2 years, inside the path of which we collaborated on 4 critical product launches") A tough reproduction is a extremely good idea for an in-individual interview, and for any later-round interview, being prepared to ship the report as quickly as you're asked for it demonstrates the way you prepared in advance.

24. Test any crucial hardware.

Check in advance of time to look that every one of the vital network connections, software program program software, and hardware are functioning well in case you are conducting your interview over the smartphone or laptop. Make fine your headphones and microphone are associated previous to the start of the interview if you can.

25. Prepare your bag earlier.

You need to deliver a handbag, backpack, or briefcase this is massive enough to healthy all your daily necessities, similarly to the necessities you need on your interview, like extra resumes and a notepad, and a unique emergency package that has the whole thing you will probably want in an emergency (count on: Breath mints, an umbrella, band-aids, and a stain stick). To make certain that you are fairly organized for an interview, here is a popular tick list. Also empty that bag! On the off hazard that you want to dig beyond treats coverings, smartphone chargers, and vintage receipts to get that resume, you may appearance pretty disrupted.

26. Determine your excursion spot and the course you can take there.

Check your path earlier, together with wherein you may park, whether or not or not or now not you're riding or taking public transportation. Fill up your tank, purchase any important tickets, add coins to your metro card, or perform a little thing else that could sluggish you down at the manner in your interview. Make positive you apprehend how long it must take you to get there and go away loads of time for web page visitors or public transportation delays.

Chapter 15: Presenting Yourself

Chapter 2 of our book specializes within the significance of building self warranty and imparting yourself successfully throughout hobby interviews. For many job seekers, interviews can be a nerve-wracking experience, filled with uncertainty and tension. However, with the proper thoughts-set and education, it's feasible to technique interviews with self belief and professionalism.

One key aspect of constructing self assurance is understanding your private strengths and qualifications. This way taking the time to mirror in your capabilities, reports, and achievements, and identifying how they align with the necessities of the approach you're using for. By doing so, you'll be better prepared to articulate your rate proposition to functionality employers, and to give your self as a sturdy candidate for the area.

Another crucial thing of supplying your self successfully is taking note of your nonverbal verbal exchange. This includes your posture, facial expressions, and gestures, in addition to your tone of voice and general demeanor. By projecting self guarantee and enthusiasm thru your body language and tone, you'll be capable of make a effective impact on functionality employers and produce your interest inside the function.

Of route, constructing self belief and providing your self correctly additionally requires exercise. This method rehearsing your responses to common interview questions, practising your nonverbal conversation in the the front of a replicate, and attempting to find comments from buddies or colleagues By doing so, you'll be able to refine your approach and collect the abilities and self assurance you want to succeed in your undertaking interviews.

Ultimately, economic wreck 2 is about empowering procedure seekers to method interviews with self perception and professionalism. By information your personal strengths and qualifications, listening to your nonverbal verbal exchange, and operating in the path of your technique, you'll be higher equipped to make a robust have an impact on on capability employers and land the task you want.

Tips for Introducing Yourself in an Interview How well you introduce yourself affects how recruiters view you as a candidate. Self-introduction is important because it offers interviewers a check your persona and presentation talents and gives you a danger to speak right now to employers approximately your talents, experience, and different accomplishments. The extremely good recommendation for responding to the query "tell us approximately yourself" inside the route of a campus placement interview may be observed right right here.

1. Begin Your Self-Introduction By greeting the interviewers, you may begin yourself-

introduction. Next, thank the interviewers for calling you to schedule the interview. Who you're and in which you live should be mentioned within the first segment of your self-creation. You want to say, "My name is Leonardo, and I'm from San Francisco," as an example.

2. If you're a state-of-the-art graduate, speak your academic historic past with the interviewers without going into more detail about your non-public data. The name of your faculty, university, or college, and your instructional degree should be said to the interviewers. If you watched it's essential, encompass your cumulative grade factor not unusual (CGPA); Otherwise, don't speak approximately grades. You ought to also talk about any duties you've worked on and any certifications you've earned which is probably related to the hobby you're using for.

three. An Alternative Strategy for Experienced Professionals Are you an expert

expert who's uncertain of how to introduce your self during an interview? If you're certainly one of them, you may right now begin talking about your most brand new challenge after greeting your interviewers and expressing your gratitude. Mention the call of the organization employer you parent for, your current emerge as privy to, the time frame you have got been employed, your characteristic, and the most important duties you take on. Feel loose to percent exciting statistics approximately your paintings accomplishments; but, you want to offer proof to decrease returned up your claims. You should, for example, claim which you have been chargeable for riding a 12 month development of 38% in customer service sentiment.

www.ingramcontent.com/pod-product-compliance
Lightning Source LLC
Chambersburg PA
CBHW071443080526
44587CB00014B/1970